CRESCENDO

CRESCENDO

THE *JAIME JORGE* STORY

Pacific Press®
Publishing Association

Nampa, Idaho | Oshawa, Ontario, Canada
www.pacificpress.com

Cover design by Gerald Lee Monks
Cover design resources from the author
Inside design by Kristin Hansen-Mellish
Inside images provided by the author

The author assumes full responsibility for the accuracy of all facts and quotations as cited in this book.

Unless otherwise noted, all scripture quotations are from The New King James Version, copyright © 1979, 1980, 1982, Thomas Nelson, Inc., Publishers.

Scripture quotations marked NIV are from the HOLY BIBLE, NEW INTERNATIONAL VERSION®. Copyright © 1973, 1978, 1984 by International Bible Society. Used by permission of Zondervan Publishing House. All rights reserved.

Additional copies of this book are available by calling toll-free 1-800-765-6955 or by visiting www.ABCasap.com.

ISBN 13: 978-0-8163-4548-9
ISBN 10: 0-8163-4548-1

13 14 15 16 17 • 5 4 3 2 1

DEDICATION

This book is dedicated to my mother, Mayda Isabel García, the person who has exerted the greatest influence in my life apart from my Savior, Jesus Christ.

As the days go by and I gain perspective on life as well as look back on my own, I am able to appreciate more and more what you've done for me and our family, and the great blessing and privilege I have to call you "Mima." You have been my greatest teacher and example. You have believed in me more than anyone else in this world has. Over and over and over again, you worked harder than what seemed humanly possible, sacrificed, persevered, and triumphed in the quest to give your family the best you could. It is you who taught me to love Jesus, to be entrepreneurial, and to dream big. Of course, you taught me so much more.

For me, there is no greater honor on this earth than to make you proud. I understand God's love a little bit better because of you!

CONTENTS

Preface			9
Chapter	1	Al Niente	13
Chapter	2	Vivace	19
Chapter	3	Con Brio	25
Chapter	4	Rallentando	31
Chapter	5	Forte Piano	35
Chapter	6	Grandioso	39
Chapter	7	Doloroso	45
Chapter	8	Tremolo	49
Chapter	9	Sempre Maestoso	57
Chapter	10	Ritardando	65
Chapter	11	Enfatico	73
Chapter	12	Sforzando	91
Chapter	13	Dolcissimo	103
Chapter	14	Legato	109
Chapter	15	Con Fuoco	115
Chapter	16	Appassionato	133
Chapter	17	Fortissimo	149
Chapter	18	Crescendo	165
Appendix		Dinner With Jaime	175

PREFACE

It took me thirty years to write my first autobiography. It's taken twelve years to write the second one—the book you are about to read. As a boy in Cuba, I remember listening in on the conversations of "old" people and how they said that time seemed to fly by as they got older. Back then, a day lasted me a week. I could do so much in a day and still have hours and hours for boredom or games or whatever I wanted to do, within reason. Now it's different. I often say in my concerts, "People say, 'Time flies when you're having fun.' But I say, 'Time flies, period! Whether you're having fun or not.'"

I was in South Africa on a safari in January 2013. Going on a safari had been a dream of mine for I don't know how many years: being as close to a lion as possible, without a cage and without getting eaten; looking into its eyes from a few feet away (in the comfort and safety of a Land Cruiser) without fear; and seeing a cheetah, a leopard (I never did see one), and the many other creatures that roam the gigantic reserves freely. I had invited a handful of people to go with me. My sister, Maydelé, couldn't go. Neither could close friends Bob Norman, Sam Ocampo, and Mark Newmyer. But Ilsa Nation could go.

I had worked on this trip for a couple of years. I had bid on and won a seven-day safari at a charity auction. The most difficult part was finding the time. I've been on a permanent tour for the last eight years—an average of three hundred days a year on the road and more than two hundred concerts a year. Now my certificate for the safari was about to expire. So I did what I hadn't done in years:

I blocked off two weeks from the concert schedule, and I planned to go on the safari. Ilsa and I worked on all the pertinent details.

Three days into the safari, I asked for her advice. She's one of the brightest and most knowledgeable people I know, and one of my best friends. I said to her, "Help me find a title for the book." I was way behind getting the manuscript to the publisher. They were running out of patience. I had worked on the storyline, but I needed a title—a good title.

The title of my first autobiography was clever—*No More Broken Strings*. It detailed my life of ups and downs, and the ending was triumphant and exciting: I had grown up physically, mentally, emotionally, and spiritually. God had delivered me over and over again from myself and from so many dangers in this life. Good things were happening all around. The sky was the limit.

And then, as the old Gilbert O'Sullivan song goes, "But as if to knock me down, reality came around, and without so much as a mere touch cut me into little pieces . . ." So much had changed in my life. So much had gone wrong. Some of it happened almost overnight; the rest had taken place slowly but surely, imperceptibly. *No More Broken Strings* now felt like a crude joke life had played on me, and I had helped the process. Sure, I had a story to tell for this second book, but it didn't have a good ending.

While on tour in Australia in 2009, I had read *Broken Music*, the autobiography of Sting, the pop-music icon. As I thought about potential book titles, that one seemed to make the most sense for my new book! In between the beautiful melodies of the inspirational hymns and songs and the elevating intricacies of the classical pieces hid someone who at times felt broken. Indeed, he *was* broken.

I had shared many of these thoughts with Ilsa. She knew many of the challenges, disappointments, and heartbreaks I had become buddies with. But she was having none of it. At every turn, she'd remind me of how much God was still doing to reach others through this broken person and violinist, how much God was blessing me, and how much He would continue to do so the closer I drew to Him.

And then it came to her: *Crescendo!* Immediately, it made sense. She said, "Name the book *Crescendo.* Give each chapter the name of a dynamic or term used in musical terminology—*piano, forte,* etc.—and share the stories that match these dynamics." It was a brilliant idea. It was perfect! I had a book title, and it allowed me to make sense of it all. And as you read, you will understand *Crescendo* is the most appropriate title for this book that now has the most amazing ending I could have asked for!

This book is centered around two themes: First, God and His amazing grace. Apart from God and His grace, I would have no reason for any of what I'm going to share with you in this book. It is because of Him that I can get up every time I fall. Indeed, He picks me up! It is because of Him and for Him that I want to keep going. It is because of Jesus Christ that I can face whatever life throws at me, knowing that He is faithful, He can overcome, and He is glorified. My greatest and most important reason for writing this book is to encourage *you*, to inspire and challenge *you* to live your life for Jesus. The second theme of this book revolves around people, relationships, and experiences. My father, mother, sister, uncle, other family members, loved ones, friends, as well as many others, have had a tremendous, vital impact on my life. As human beings, we seek friendship and companionship. We need to be needed. We long to be wanted, appreciated, and cherished. I often say that the relationships I have with family and friends are my most prized possessions on this earth. Money comes and goes, as does status, reputation, and influence. But the bonds of family and friendship cannot be bought or sold. And experiences paint the pictures on the canvas of our lives.

This book is not about accomplishments. The world we live in seems to be fixated on things such as celebrity, star power, Hollywood, and so on. I've been to concerts where the musician spent most of the time talking about all the important, powerful, and influential people he'd performed for. I've heard sermons in which the preacher recited a Bible text or some noble principle and then proceeded to recount stories about having advised this president or having been sought after by some high-ranking politician for camaraderie or consultation (most of it is highly exaggerated or downright fabricated, and I know it). I roll my eyes. Some sincere people in the audience eat it up like it's filet mignon (or red pepper hummus, if you're vegan).

As much as possible, I will stay away from highlighting the "important" people I might have played for or interacted with. And if I have to make mention of a person's title, it's only to try to make a much more important observation about a life experience. And that life experience will always bring me back to this book's first theme—God and His amazing grace.

So enter these pages, the hallways, the dark and open rooms of the labyrinth of this book (a.k.a. my life), expecting to come out at the end of the tunnel knowing that my story is *your* story. It's the story of just about anyone who's ever walked on this earth. Because no matter how broken we may be, we have a God of second chances, of new beginnings, of hope and assurance, and of victory in Jesus. Yes, God *is* love!

Jaime with gospel music legend and friend, Del Delker.

Jaime with Take 6 before a concert in Atlanta in 2011.

CHAPTER 1
AL NIENTE
{Fade to Silence}

I arrived home in Cleveland, Tennessee, on Sunday night, September 9, 2001. The last five days had been spent in Washington and Idaho. In Washington, I had concerts in Wenatchee, Moses Lake, Spokane, and Spangle, followed by a concert in Sandpoint, Idaho. One of the most difficult, and important, pieces of a successful music ministry (unless you're signed to a label) is having a booking agent. My friend, Dan Pabón, had helped me in this regard for a while. Linda Hill, who's like a second mom to me, had done it for a few years, and a handful of others had tried their hand at it. But they all had regular jobs. Whether part time or full time, everyone worked. And they worked hard. So they just couldn't schedule my concerts and represent me full time. And I understood; there wasn't enough money in it to make a career out of it.

Several years before, I had met Herman Harp. Herman was an excellent musician who sang as a soloist; as a duo with his wife, Sonnie; and with the group Ponder, Harp, and Jennings. But this guy was a workhorse like few people I'd ever seen! He put on 250–300 concerts a year. And when he decided to schedule my concerts, he used the vast database of the thousands of churches he had sung in to help me. He brought me to another level so that a typical weekend, from Thursday or Friday evening until Sunday evening, would have four concerts or more.

I also had another booking agent, Peggy Buhr, at Adoration Resources in Kansas City, Missouri. My manager, Mark Craig, had suggested Peggy and I work together, since one of the artists she represented was also an instrumentalist whom

Mark managed. So over the course of the next few years, while I had two book-ing agents, it wouldn't be unusual for Herman to book a couple of concerts in, say, Southern California from Friday night to Saturday night, while Peggy would book me in, say, Houston, Texas, for Sunday. This would happen when both of them would get calls for concerts at about the same time. So I'd do the concerts in Southern California, dash to Los Angeles International Airport (LAX) to catch a midnight flight, and arrive in Houston in time to play special music for the morning church service and/or put on the evening concert. Of course, this made for one tired dude at the end of the weekend! But I thrived on these opportunities to share the talents God has entrusted to me, and I must say, I thrived on the adventure of accomplishing the feat. More than once I came within minutes of missing a flight. As you can imagine, it would have been a disaster to not make it to a concert. Amazingly (more likely, providentially), I never missed a concert.

But the weekend of September 7–9, 2001, was a fairly benign one in terms of getting to all the concerts because I was in one area of the country and had to drive only a relatively short distance from one place to the next. On Sunday, I had to get home instead of taking a Sunday evening concert because the next day I had a concert at the corporate headquarters of Life Care Centers of America (LCCA), which had gathered its directors of nurses from all over the country for a training session. This would turn out to be the first of many concerts for LCCA and the beginning of a relationship with that wonderful organization that continues today.

I arrived at the Chattanooga airport, and my wife, Emily, picked me up. I was exhausted after a long weekend of concerts, but grateful and anxious to come home to Emily and our apartment in Cleveland, Tennessee. I was also excited about the fantastic reception and response the concerts had received.

Monday, September 10, was like any other time I returned home from a con-cert trip—unpacking, taking inventory of the products sold, going to the bank and the dry cleaners, and spending time with Emily. The facility where the LCCA concert was to take place was about ten minutes from our apartment, so we were able to finish all our errands and still have plenty of time to get ready. Emily had cut back a bit on traveling with me, so it was a bonus to have her there.

We arrived, and the friendly and helpful LCCA staff made sure our sound check and setup was easy and quick. I was introduced to Forrest Preston and his wife, Kathleen, and Beecher Hunter and his wife, Lola. These men were the chairman of the board and chief operating officer, respectively of LCCA, and they welcomed us and made us feel at home. I was impressed with the way every staff member carried himself or herself. The staff was kind, cordial, easy to work with, and there was an atmosphere of joy and peace.

In my concerts, I always have a set of songs and pieces ready to play, and I like to arrive at the venue and observe people, or even interact with some, before put-ting together the program. This evening was no different. I decided to mix some inspirational songs with classical and patriotic music and then finish with a hymn and a spiritual emphasis. Life Care Centers of America is an organization with a Christian emphasis and environment, and I had been told that I could share my faith without any issues at all.

For the last song, I chose a medley of "The Star-Spangled Banner," "The Battle Hymn of the Republic," and "America the Beautiful." I had attended a concert in 1986 by Sam Ocampo, someone who became a great inspiration, mentor, and friend. Toward the end of that concert on a cold Michigan night, he had performed a medley of these same songs. I was fifteen years old at the time, and as the music rose to a crescendo, I had tears in my eyes and goose bumps on top of goose bumps. I was in awe of what Sam could do with that piano. Without him saying a word, the notes emanating from the keys as his fingers played, spoke to me with clarity and precision. And so when I recorded the album *I Am Not Worthy* in 1994, I included a medley of these three patriotic songs that was very much based on Sam's version.

Every concert for me is special, different, and exciting. But some concerts stand out for different reasons—some good, some not so good. This LCCA concert stood out. Everything seemed to be going right—the sound was perfect; the lighting was just right; the audience was attentive. Even in a place and setting that wasn't really to be a gospel-style concert, the Holy Spirit was present. For some reason, as I shared with the audience something of my family's story and my love for the United States of America, I felt impressed to go a bit further and challenge the audience to be ever thankful for the freedoms, blessings, opportunities, and liberties we enjoy, and to use them wisely to serve God and humanity. People were visibly moved. After the enthusiastic response of those present died down, Beecher Hunter came up on stage, said a few words, and invited me to share one more song. This gave me an excellent opportunity to close with a favorite hymn, "How Great Thou Art," and end on a very spiritual note.

As Emily and I greeted people after the concert, nobody knew or understood the impact this patriotic medley would leave in the hearts and minds of those present in the light of what happened just twelve hours later in New York, Washington, D.C., Pennsylvania, and, indeed, around the world.

The morning of September 11, 2001, began just like any other morning for millions, perhaps even billions, of people around the world. Emily and I woke up and had our worship and prayer. We were going about routine things when my buddy, Trent DeLong, called me on the phone. It was difficult to keep track of Trent's whereabouts because he was constantly traveling and doing concerts. If he was at home in California that day, he must have been calling me just after 6:00 A.M. his time. But he was the first person I heard it from. He said to me, "Turn on the television. An airplane has just slammed into the World Trade Center in New York, and there's chaos all around." So Emily rushed to turn on the television, and we watched in shock, horror, and despair as the events we all know and remember unfolded.

This country and, indeed, the world would never be the same. At the time, we could not comprehend or imagine how things would change, but we knew they would. We prayed for our country, for the thousands of people whose lives were tragically ended, for the families of those who lost loved ones in the blink of an eye, and for the millions who'd be affected one way or another by all this.

Being a frequent flier, I could imagine the uncertainty and inconvenience so many people experienced as the entire air traffic system in the United States was halted. I could have easily been stranded somewhere, as much as I fly. People were stuck for days and days. I learned later that LCCA chartered buses to drive home those nurse directors I had played for on Monday night. I had a presentation in Missouri on Friday night, September 15, and another one in Georgia the following night. The organizers of the Friday night event canceled the function, but the one in Atlanta proceeded.

In Tennessee, mail delivery was shut down for three days. Perhaps it did so in other areas of the country as well, and most airports were closed. The stock market dropped like an iron ball, and the economy immediately took a dive. It was a time for our nation to reflect and pray. I remember noticing an increase in attendance at churches all around the country; people were looking for answers.

Emily and I were two months away from purchasing our first home, and, of course, with the new economic instability, we were anxious about this huge commitment.

One week later, on September 18, I boarded an American Eagle jet headed to Chicago and then caught a connecting flight to LAX on American Airlines. The Chattanooga airport isn't a busy airport to begin with, but on this day, it felt like a museum at midnight. There were a handful of passengers at all the counters, and the mood was somber and hushed. In the months following September 11, there would be long, winding lines of people waiting for hours to get through security, but that morning it took me less than two minutes. There were six passengers on my flight. When I arrived at Chicago O'Hare International Airport, I thought I was at Chicago Midway International Airport! (That's a facetious comment; those who know Chicago well and the bad blood between the two airports will understand!) There were fourteen passengers on the McDonnell Douglas Super 80 aircraft; normally passengers would have been waitlisted to get on the flight to Los Angeles.

Perhaps the worst part was that everyone everywhere looked at everyone else with suspicion. Everyone was scared and apprehensive. A loud bang or unusual sound would make people jump, and when the airport's security staff suddenly announced a halt in movement to investigate a possible security breach, everyone froze and recoiled in fear. It was painful to see a nation of people who were now stressed and uncertain.

I arrived in Los Angeles and drove to Stockton for my first concert, which would take place the next night. After that, I drove back to the Los Angeles area for concerts the rest of the weekend in Palm Desert and Los Angeles proper. The last presentation that weekend was a bit impromptu and mostly unplanned. In 1999, I had been booked to do a Christmas concert at the White Memorial Medical Center. This hospital, located on Cesar Chavez Avenue in the heart of East Los Angeles, serves the humble community surrounding it. It carries out its mission faithfully, giving health care and spiritual healing to many who cannot afford the care they receive. When Emily and I arrived there in 1999, we were given a tour of the hospital and met the patients and staff. We fell in love with the people, the place, and the mission. I've returned there many times to do presentations, speak, and play along the hallways of the hospital for the patients and staff.

One of the people Emily and I met that weekend was Mark Newmyer, the hospital's vice president for business development. He and his wife, Helena, entertained us throughout the weekend, and Emily and I were thankful for the time and interest Mark and Helena took in us. I'm honored to say that Mark has become one of my closest friends.

That Sunday evening, September 23, 2001, the hospital was putting on its yearly gala at the Beverly Hilton Hotel. Mark had invited me to attend the gala as his guest. Because of his responsibilities, he had to be there early, and I went with him. As the afternoon progressed, I sensed angst and anxiety on the part of the organizers. Shari Davis of SD Events, producer of the gala and a brilliant lady, was pacing back and forth, on and off her cell phone, and going from one person to the next, talking. I didn't know it, but the band booked to provide the entertainment for the evening had not shown up, and the gala was scheduled to begin in less than two hours. As a violinist, I have a sweet deal—I don't have lots of complicated equipment I have to bring or set up (besides my microphone, iPhone, iPad, or MacBook Pro), and I don't have to spend an hour or more doing a sound check. Of course, I'm at the mercy of the equipment that the local venue has and the audio and video engineers that are provided. I typically show up an hour and a half before a concert, take about twenty or thirty minutes to do a sound check, and then I can go do other things—review last-minute details, signals, order of the program, and so on, with the audio and video engineers, set up, get dressed, pray with the prayer team, and relax until it's time to begin the concert.

Finally, Mark came over to tell me what was going on. Things were getting desperate. The band, even if they showed up now, would need plenty of time to set up, and the starting time for the gala couldn't be delayed. So Mark told Shari he had a friend who played the violin and could pinch-hit. I could only imagine Shari's thoughts (which she confirmed later): *How many times have I heard, "I know someone who's a great musician," and then when it's time to play, the musician isn't great at all?* She was skeptical of Mark's friend. And so in the midst of the chaos, I was asked to play a song on stage. Of course, this was their way of auditioning me. And I'm sure they planned for the worst.

I ran out to the car to get my violin. Returning, I handed them a CD track of

"God Bless the U.S.A.," the song made famous by Lee Greenwood. They cranked up the music and set up a microphone for me. We adjusted the volume of the monitor speakers, and I began playing. As I played, I noticed, Shari, her assistants, and a couple of others who had been hopping around were slowing down and huddling together. I then drifted into the music and got lost in it, tuning out everything else around me. Suddenly, the accompaniment stopped. I had become so involved in the melody that I was almost jolted when the music stopped, feeling a bit disoriented. At that point, I didn't know what to think. Then, Shari came over and asked me, "Can you provide about an hour's worth of music?"

"Yes," I said. "No problem."

From that point on, the running around ceased. I was assigned an assistant and a dressing room, and plans continued smoothly.

Later that evening, I learned that not twenty minutes after I was invited to play, the band showed up. Apparently, they thought the event was in another hotel and then got lost. But nobody had heard from them. So when they arrived, they were told that they had not honored the agreement and that they had been replaced. You can imagine how well that went. The next year, both the band *and* I were invited to participate at the gala!

CHAPTER 2

VIVACE
{Very Lively; Up Tempo}

I t was probably two days after 9/11 that I received a phone call from Milagros Tomei, a friend who worked at the corporate headquarters of Coca-Cola in Atlanta. I had met Milagros a couple of years before. She had been a faithful supporter of a ministry I was working with that was involved in God's work in Cuba, but I didn't know she worked for Coca-Cola. As it turned out, she was a midlevel executive. She told me that the company wanted to put together a special concert for its employees with a patriotic theme. They were looking for artists, and Milagros recommended me. Coca-Cola is one of the top companies in the world, so I was excited to have the opportunity to perform for it, particularly because I was proud of the fact that the former chairman and chief executive officer of the company, Roberto Goizueta, had been born in Cuba. He had come to this country with nothing and had risen to lead Coca-Cola to the pinnacle of corporate success. Sadly, he was a chain smoker, and his life was cut short because of lung cancer in 1997.

The company wanted two concerts on Friday, September 28, called "A Coca-Cola Salute to America," so I had to rearrange my flights, because I already had concerts scheduled for later that weekend in the Boise, Idaho, area. Since the invitation had come directly to me, I asked my manager, Mark, to handle all the details of the performance.

Emily flew out to Boise on Friday. On Thursday afternoon, I drove down to Atlanta to meet with the organizers of the Coca-Cola concert. I was absolutely amazed at the security around the corporate headquarters—layers of gates with security checkpoints. At one stop, they even inspected underneath my car! Eventually, I made it inside the building, and Marc Nevarez, the associate event manager greeted me. He gave me a quick tour of a few areas. (The building is beautiful, and the décor is attractively all things Coca-Cola!) We went to the auditorium where the concert was to take place—the Roberto C. Goizueta Auditorium. We had a sound check and discussed every aspect of each program. At that point, someone told me that they did not want me to talk about religion or God and that any reference to faith should be kept to a minimum.

When we were finished, I headed to the Atlanta Four Seasons Hotel to spend the night. Now, let me tell you, I don't often stay in a Four Seasons hotel; actually, this was my first time. The room was so spectacular that I sat in every chair, lay in every inch of that splendidly comfortable bed, and wore both bathrobes hanging in the closet (not at the same time). After a while, of course, I became accustomed to the room, practiced my violin, carefully crafted the program, went to the gym for a workout, and turned in for the night.

The next morning, I arrived at the headquarters early to get through all the security checks. I made my way to the front of the building where Marc was waiting for me, and we headed to the auditorium. I burned the CD with all the accompaniment tracks, prepared the video to go along with the patriotic medley (the same recorded version I had played a couple of weeks before at LCCA), and prayed with vocalist Yvette Figueroa, the other artist participating in this Salute to America concert.

The utter efficiency and exactitude with which everything was organized and carried out left an indelible impression on my mind. David Quillin, the production manager, made sure every aspect of the sound, video, lighting, and stage was perfectly prepared. Holly Formel, the logistics lead, and Robyn Downin, a member of the logistics team, had all of the behind-the-scenes details taken care of. And Chuck Millirons, the production lead, took time to talk with me and make sure I was comfortable.

The first program at 11:00 A.M. was a rousing success. Hundreds of Coca-Cola employees filled the auditorium, and they were inspired and encouraged. The 4:30 P.M. program ran a little late, but nobody minded. I remember leaving a bit concerned. On one hand, the performance had been everything I had hoped for, and the response the same. On the other hand, I felt a bit empty. Here I had played my heart out and people were excited, yet I was not able to share with them what was most important to me—Jesus. I had managed to mention a few things about my faith and convictions. In fact, I was surprised when several of the employees came up to talk after each program and said things such as, "You're a believer, aren't you? I can tell." Or, "I know God is with you. Thank you for your witness." But I didn't feel completely happy. As I drove home and took in the sunset and the beauty and majesty of northern Georgia and Tennessee, I asked the

Lord to give me more opportunities to be in places where I could not only play music that honored Him but also to be able to speak about Him more. I told Him I did not want to be lured by opportunities that, although they paid more than church concerts, didn't allow me to witness for Him.

The next morning my first flight was at 6:00 a.m. I had to get on three planes to reach my destination—Chattanooga to Chicago, Chicago to Seattle, and Seattle to Boise. I arrived in Boise a little late, waited for my bags, and headed to the car rental lot to get my car. I was rushing around because I still had to go to the hotel, pick up Emily, get dressed, and head for the evening concert.

Back then, you could carry a lot more weight in your luggage than today, so I didn't exactly travel light! I would check a garment bag with my clothes and equipment, along with a suitcase containing all the products for the concerts (cassettes, CDs, DVDs, etc.), with my violin and briefcase as carry-ons. So imagine me walking up and down airports, on escalators and moving walkways, with a rolling suitcase in my left hand, a rolling garment bag in my right, my briefcase on my left shoulder, and my violin on my right shoulder. Not exactly Speedy Gonzales zipping through an airport!

These were the days before Bluetooth headsets, and as I began laboring from the rental car counter to the lot, my cell phone rang. Emily was calling me to let me know she was ready and that we needed to strategize as to who would do what when we arrived at the church, because we would get there only about thirty minutes before the concert began. I didn't want to wait until getting in the car to talk to her, so I put down my briefcase to answer the phone. Then using my shoulder to press the cell phone against my ear, I continued my slow trek. I arrived at my car, stuffed my things in the trunk and back seat, and began to drive away. As I did so, still talking with Emily, I had this vague recollection of looking in the rearview mirror and seeing a rental car company agent waving her arms at me. I thought it was strange, and I drove away. As I drove down Interstate 84, going as fast as I could and trying to stay under the speed limit, I had a wicked thought: *Where's my briefcase?* Everything came together at that moment—the woman waving her arms at me when I drove away was holding my briefcase and trying to get my attention. I was horrified! This was seventeen days after 9/11. You couldn't leave a candy wrapper unattended around an airport. The audio recordings in every airport repeated the same words over the intercom: "Please do not leave any baggage unattended." If you left your bag somewhere, it could be confiscated, destroyed, and you could be fined. And, of course, my briefcase was full of important things: my Bible, computer, passport, wallet, documents, and so on. In fact, I was bringing the nearly completed manuscript for my book *No More Broken Strings* to Susan Harvey, a vice president of Pacific Press®, to put the finishing editing touches on it.

In a panic, I took the nearest exit and turned around. I sped back toward the airport, this time going so fast I was definitely under grace and not under the law. I prayed and begged the Lord that nothing would happen to my briefcase. About twelve minutes later, I arrived at the rental car lot. I was frantically walking around when I recognized the agent who had tried to stop me earlier. She figured out who I was immediately. She smiled and said, "I tried to get your attention as you drove away, but you didn't see me. You don't look like a terrorist, so I kept the bag here with me." I didn't know quite what to make of her comment, but I thanked this wonderful lady as she gave me the briefcase. Of course, my heart was racing and we arrived barely in time for the concert, but by the grace of God, everything was all right.

The next day we had a concert at the Nampa First Church of the Nazarene. I must say that concert came about in one of the most unorthodox ways I've ever had a concert scheduled! About a year before, when I was visiting my friends Warren Gough and Randy Maxwell at Pacific Press®, they took me to meet the minister of music of this church. I wasn't all that excited about this, because I could imagine how uncomfortable the pastor, Mike Wiebe, might feel to have someone bring over an artist and say, "This guy is good; you need to book him to do a concert at your church." So half embarrassed and half squirming in my shoes, I drove over with them to the Nazarene church office.

When we arrived, everyone began to talk cordially. And then Warren not only introduced me to Pastor Mike and sang my praises, but he also asked me to take out my violin and play for the pastor. I wanted to disappear at that moment! I inspected Pastor Mike's expression to see any trace of discomfort, at which point I'd have found a way to break a string or something so that I couldn't play. But he didn't flinch. So I took out my fiddle, inserted a CD with my accompaniment tracks in his stereo, and played something. Obviously he was pleased because he scheduled me for a concert at his church—and has done so more than once since.

In November 2001, I was in Springfield, Illinois, for some concerts. Peggy had scheduled me to do one sponsored by the Fleming Academy of the Performing Arts. This is a thriving Suzuki school of strings, led by its dedicated founder, Trudy Fleming. The purpose of the concert was twofold: (1) to encourage and inspire the dozens of students in the academy, and (2) to bless the parents of the students as well as the community. Trudy arranged the concert to take place at a local church, the Springfield First Church of the Nazarene, and then I had been invited to minister the next morning during the worship service.

I arrived there Saturday evening and proceeded to practice with the performers and set up everything else necessary for the event. The church filled nicely, and the concert began. I remember the concert very well. Not only could I sense the excitement and enthusiasm in these precious little violinists but also God's Spirit began to move. Toward the end of the concert, I looked upstairs in the balcony, and I saw a couple just praising the Lord. Afterward, that same couple came and talked to me. As it turned out, the gentleman was the senior pastor of the church. The next day we witnessed a similar work being done by the Holy Spirit as lives were touched and transformed. Pastor Tim and Vicky Gates welcomed me with open arms, and we have been friends ever since. In fact, I've had the honor of being invited to every church Tim has pastored since then—the Texarkana, Texas, First Church of the Nazarene and the St. Cloud, Florida, Church of the Nazarene. Some time ago, Vicky was diagnosed with cancer. But the Lord still has plans for her, and she has gone into remission. Praise the Lord for the ways in which He still works in people's lives today!

CHAPTER 3

CON BRIO
{With Vigor}

O n November 19, 2001, Emily and I signed papers for and moved into our first house. Until that point, we had lived in two humble apartments—one in Shelby, North Carolina (from 1997 to 2000) and another in Cleveland, Tennessee (from 2000 to 2001). Our apartments were small and cozy, and we were very happy. But the Lord had blessed His music ministry and us abundantly, and we were now ready to take the step of home ownership. I was pretty much a city slicker, having lived in cities such as Milwaukee and Chicago most of my life. Emily was a different story. She had spent many years on a farm in Arkansas, and she wasn't a big fan of cities. She would recount the happy days when she could roam around her parents' property and see the cows her dad raised. I remember visiting the home of Dad Estle and Mom Delores (or Dee) and enjoying the surroundings. And I've got to tell you, those cows were the happiest cows I've ever seen! When Dad Estle went anywhere near those cows, they flocked to him. He treated them well and fed them with such care that they had to be in cow heaven! I've never forgotten that.

When Emily and I felt ready to buy a house and began looking, people advised us to buy something simple, maybe a fixer-upper. But I'm no Handy-Andy. Besides, one nail through my finger while trying to put in a floor or a board, and my career as a musician might be over. I've never been very patient, and I don't like to do things halfway. So after we looked around at these simple houses and fixer-uppers, we decided this route wasn't for us. Then we found a house that was just going up in a beautiful neighborhood on a mountain outside Chattanooga. We could not change the floor plan, but we could have plenty of input on the materials, colors, patterns, and so forth.

My creativity is limited mostly to music. I'm not the type of person who can decorate a room with matching furniture. I can tell you if I love it or if I don't! But Emily is a different story. We would walk into a furniture store, and as she went through several rooms, she'd point and say, "This piece goes here; that one goes there, and this piece goes over there." My head spun trying to understand this gift and capacity she had. So I left her to choose the furniture for the new house. And she did a beautiful job! It was going to be a lengthy project to furnish the whole place, but at least we had what we needed to move in and make the place home.

Our builder, Frank Basadre, had been pressed by the bank to complete the house by a certain date in order to qualify for the loan; and so for the first few months, there were a lot of kinks that had to be worked out—nails coming out of doors, water dripping from an air vent, paint cracking outside, and so on. But I understand that these things are not uncommon when you move into a newly built house.

I still remember that first night in our new home. We were so happy and thankful to the Lord for working out all the details. We now had our own place. Of course, we really didn't. The bank owned it, and it would be ours only when we had made a couple of hundred (or more) monthly payments. For weeks after we moved in, I was so excited I couldn't sleep when we went to bed. When I was certain that Emily was sleeping soundly, I would get up and walk all around the house, marveling, asking myself if this was real. It was. And I thought over and over about the fact that God is so good. Of course, God's blessings should never be measured in terms of finances or material things. They are so much more than that. And Emily and I praised the Lord for giving us so much in so many areas.

That first Thanksgiving and Christmas were beautiful moments we were able to spend with family and friends. We had both dreamed of having a place where we could have people over and have enough space to comfortably host everyone without some having to stay in hotels. So we cherished these holidays. Our home became a place where many came, stayed, visited, and enjoyed.

Emily had finished her bachelor of science in nursing degree in 1997 and had done some as-needed nursing work in North Carolina and Tennessee. During the first three years of our marriage, she traveled quite a bit with me. But anyone who's traveled a lot knows that it's not as glamorous as many people think. It's one thing to travel once in a while. It's quite another to do so for a living. I remember that before September 11, I could arrive at an airport (depending on the size) as late as thirty minutes before a flight and comfortably board without any problem. After 9/11, everything changed. Sometimes, I could arrive an hour and a half before the flight and have no problem. Other times, three hours might not be enough. So during the first two or three years after 9/11, traveling became absolute torture.

As a result, Emily began to scale back on travel. Also, sudden changes in climate, temperature, and weather conditions seemed to trigger her asthma, and that didn't help either. The profession she had chosen—nursing—was not something she had a passion for. She was frustrated to have gone to school for four years, obtained a degree, but did not really enjoy her career. Emily is a true artist. Her ability to create and decorate, not to mention interpret music, is absolutely astounding. For some of our family gatherings at Thanksgiving or Christmas, she would prepare interactive games, plan outings, and put together other activities that made our time together enjoyable and informative. At one point, she began making gorgeous wreaths that sold for hundreds of dollars in consignment shops. I began to sense that she needed to have an outlet for all this creativity.

At the age of nineteen Emily had been one of two young ladies, out of several hundred, who were offered a modeling contract by Elite New York, and she had declined it. She was smart to do so, because she was in college. But now, she gave modeling a try. She was probably too old to land big gigs (modeling agencies start these girls around thirteen or fourteen years old these days), but she began pursuing this avenue. She began to appear in local and regional advertising campaigns, even spending quite a bit of time working in New York in 2002. In the fall, she spent more than a month modeling in Milan, Italy, where she was quite successful.

In the spring of 2002, through her modeling jobs, she was invited to go to Nashville and appear in the music video of a country music singer-songwriter. That was a pretty exciting opportunity, and she returned home with an even greater possibility—the artist was willing to help her have the chance to establish a singing career. Emily's greatest talent is undoubtedly music. Though she didn't study music formally, she has a sensitivity, an affinity, and a natural ability to feel, interpret, and write music that is truly special. It can only be understood to be a gift from God. She came to talk to me about pursuing a career in country music, and I told her I was happy to support her. Without question, it was going to be tricky on a number of fronts. She would have to spend a lot of time in Nashville by herself; we were going to spend more time apart than we already were, and she was going to be functioning in a very different world—the world of entertainment.

I thought about this opportunity for her. I agonized over it and prayed long and hard about her decision. I wanted her to pursue her passion, but I also didn't want us to be apart more than we already were. Looking back now, it's easy to think that I, or we, made the wrong decision. But I told her I'd do everything I could to support her and make it possible for her to give it a shot. I also told her if she made it, I'd learn to be a fiddler and play in her band!

When Herman Harp slowed down his torrid pace of traveling and concerts, he booked concerts for me. But when he decided to hit the road with a vengeance, I had to find someone else. I approached the wife of my boss and friend, Dr. Frank González, the speaker-director of La Voz de la Esperanza. I asked her if she would be willing to book concerts for me. She asked me what it entailed, and I explained it to her. I needed someone who is organized, very professional, and long-suffering. (A great deal of patience is needed sometimes to work with the different churches, personalities, and needs of various places.) I needed someone methodical and motivated. (Sometimes it takes quite a long time to connect with people and get things going.) And I needed someone who is a good communicator, who would make and receive calls with the goal of filling my schedule with opportunities to minister, share, witness, and make a living at music ministry. Most of all, I needed someone who believes in what she is doing.

One of the people who believed in me was Linda Hill. I had met her, her husband, Herb, and their children, Kim and James, when I lived in Chicago in the early 1990s. At the time, Linda was working for an organization that provided support to cancer survivors. Somehow, she got hold of my phone number and called me to play for one of her organization's functions. I was in college at the time, so I wasn't in full-time music ministry. I wound up becoming very good friends with Linda and her family. I worked part time for her one summer before I graduated from college, taught violin to her son, James, and through the years spent quite a bit of time with the family. Linda believed in me! Her husband was an executive specializing in human resources; and when he got a job doing that in a hospital in Hastings, Nebraska, the family moved there. Linda managed the bookstore at a college in Lincoln, which was probably a sixty-to-eighty-hour-a-week job!

But despite that, Linda told me she felt impressed to help grow God's music ministry. And so despite the long hours she put in at the bookstore, she would make phone calls and get me concerts and appearances. And she wouldn't take No for an answer! She managed to get me into churches that had not previously scheduled me. And this is how I met Mark Craig, my manager. Mark produced the National Religious Broadcasters yearly convention for more than twenty years. Of course, having the opportunity to perform at a gathering like that is sweet indeed, and so far I had not been able to get in. Well, in 2000, Linda reached Mark on the phone. At first, Mark told her that he had all the music he needed for that year's convention. But she didn't give up. She spoke to him more than once until he acquiesced and found me a slot. It wasn't glamorous, but I played for a function where there were a number of prominent pastors and leaders present. One of them was Dr. Tony Evans, who asked for my information afterward in order to invite me to do a concert at his church.

Sometime after the convention, Mark called me, having heard some of my recordings, and asked if I was interested in having him manage me. I was, and Mark represented me for a number of years.

Unfortunately for me, Linda's husband, Herb, was offered a job working for Sanitarium Health Foods in Australia. So Herb and Linda moved to Australia for several years. But even while there, she helped build my ministry. She scheduled four concert tours to Australia and New Zealand while she was there!

But I've digressed! After Linda left for Australia, Herman and Peggy booked my concerts. After Herman went back on the road, Evelyn and Peggy did so until Peggy retired and Evelyn took over completely.

In October 2002, I found myself in the midst of a weekend where I had concerts in Indiana and Texas scheduled by two agents. I don't know if I've mentioned this, but I am *not* a morning person! I tend to be a night owl, therefore I don't function very well in the morning, especially early! But I had to get up early this particular morning to catch my flight. I managed to do that without a problem. I was still half asleep when I arrived at the Dallas/Fort Worth International Airport. My friend, Trent DeLong, who as I mentioned before, traveled constantly and was likely to be anywhere anytime, was in the area, and we had planned to hang out together for a couple of days. So I collected my luggage and went outside to wait for him. It was a cool, brisk Sunday morning, and the cool air helped me wake up a bit. Trent showed up a few minutes later, we hugged one another, put my things in his rental car, and headed to the rental car facility to return his vehicle and pick up mine.

Can you guess where this is going?

As we were transferring my bags from his car to mine, I noticed there were only three—my garment bag, suitcase, and violin. Where was my briefcase? I had brought it on the plane with me, and I remembered having it with me when I got off the plane. So where was it? I must have left it at the bench outside at the airport. We quickly finished transferring bags and cars, checked out of the rental car lot, and zoomed back to the terminal (once again at speeds that qualified us to be under grace, not under the law). It had probably been twenty or twenty-five minutes since we had left the terminal. As we arrived at the place where Trent had picked me up, the area seemed eerily empty.

We stopped right in front of the entrance. Just before Trent stopped the car and I got out, my cell phone rang. It registered an unknown number. Typically, I don't answer when that happens. But I did at that moment. When I said, "Hello," a female voice on the other end said, "Is this Mr. Jaime Jorge?"

"Yes," I responded.

"Sir," the voice continued, "this is [she gave her name] from American Airlines. Are you missing something?"

"Oh, yes," I replied anxiously.

She then explained, "Please come to counter such-and-such immediately."

I told her I would. I hopped out of the car and ran toward the automatic doors. The woman's counter was right inside. As the doors opened and I entered, she must have figured out who I was because the expression on my face was angst-ridden. I looked around, and she waved at me. I ran toward her. She was standing behind the counter, but I could see my briefcase to one side by the scale. When I saw it, I began to relax.

When I arrived at the counter, I said, "I'm Jaime Jorge." She asked for my identification, and I showed it to her. Then she told me what had just transpired. She told me that when I left my bag there and drove away, someone alerted the police. Law enforcement cordoned off the immediate area and brought in a bomb-sniffing dog to smell the bag. When they determined there was nothing dangerous in it, the officer was going to take the bag with him. But this agent, who had been standing behind the cordon, noticed that hanging on the side of the briefcase was my American Airlines Executive Platinum luggage tag. So she went over to the police officer and told him she was willing to take responsibility for the bag and explained why.

When he turned the bag over to her, she went to her computer, entered my frequent flier number into the system, and my profile came up. The only phone number showing on the profile was my home number. So she called that number. Emily answered and gave her my cell phone number. That's how she reached me as I was coming back to the terminal!

I apologized profusely for my forgetfulness. As she handed me the briefcase, she said, "Sir, please don't leave your bag unattended anymore."

"Yes, ma'am!" I replied sheepishly.

As we drove away, Trent and I thanked the Lord for keeping me from yet another disaster! I also thought about something: I was fortunate because I had my luggage tag that helped identify me. But God doesn't need a computer system or a filing cabinet in order to find us! He is always there, ready to hear us, ready to reach out to us, ready to help us when we need Him.

Trent and I arrived in Jacksonville, Texas, for my presentation at the First Baptist Church. The special program that the senior pastor, Grady Higgs, had organized for the senior adults was a great blessing and inspiration to many. Pastor Grady invited me back again to his church; and when he was called to be the executive director of the Baptist Missionary Association of America, he invited me on several occasions to participate in other activities. I have the privilege of calling Pastor Grady a friend.

CHAPTER 4

RALLENTANDO
{Progressively Slower}

Toward the end of 2002, I began to notice that my linear scleroderma had returned. In 1995, when Dr. Falanga told me that the disease had apparently gone into remission, he also told me that I would very likely have bouts of it every seven to ten years for the rest of my life. It had been seven long years since the nightmare had ended. So when I began to notice the skin on my cheek becoming thinner, I kind of freaked out. What was I going to do? How much damage was it going to do this time?

The first time around, the thing ate into my forehead, came down the side of my nose, and worked its way around my right cheek. Thank God it had not affected the muscles in my right eye or I could have lost my vision there. Now I noticed that the disease (also known as "en coup de sabre" when it affects the head as it did in my case) picked up where it had left off last time. I told Emily, and she became quite concerned. She did some research to find places that specifically treated linear scleroderma, but, of course, our insurance didn't cover any of those types of treatments offered at those clinics.

And so I went to see some doctors. One was Dr. Baroi in Southern California, and the other was right in Chattanooga near our home (alas, I can't remember his name now). Both were rheumatologists, and both suggested a pretty aggressive path to possibly arrest the illness before it gained strength. But the thought of taking large doses of methotrexate and prednisone (which I had taken previously) did not appeal to me at all. I remembered how the prednisone wreaked havoc with my metabolism, energy, and emotions. I spent quite a long time trying to decide what course of action to take. I didn't want to tell my parents, because I didn't want to worry them, especially my mom. I dragged my feet, keeping a close eye on my face, hoping that I wasn't just imagining it all. Of course, I wasn't.

I also spent a great deal of time in reflection and prayer. And I wondered why the disease had returned. I remembered coming home from medical school at the University of Illinois one day in early 1995, feeling exhausted and overwhelmed. I had so much studying to do, I simply felt discouraged. So I decided to spend some time studying God's Word and praying before I tackled the books. I opened my Bible, and it happened to open to the first chapter of the book of Daniel. Now, Daniel is one of my favorite Bible characters, so I decided to read the entire book. It's not a long book, and it's a very interesting read.

The passages and stories were, of course, very familiar. Daniel and his friends had stood faithfully for God over and over again, and God had delivered them and used them to affect many lives. As I read into chapters 9 and 10, I noticed something very interesting. In chapter 9, Gabriel says to Daniel, "At the beginning of your supplications the command went out, and I have come to tell you, for you are greatly beloved" (verse 23). I continued reading into chapter 10: "O Daniel, man greatly beloved . . ." (verse 11), and again in verse 19, "O man greatly beloved, fear not!" At that point, I realized there was a phrase that kept reappearing in these verses. I was impressed that God kept referring to Daniel as being "greatly beloved." I know that God loves us all very much. But I didn't recall other places in the Bible where God referred to other individuals as being "greatly beloved." So I decided to find out why.

I asked the Holy Spirit to explain this to me, and I went back to the beginning of chapter 1. As I reread these stories, I began to understand! Daniel was someone very different than most people in his day and age. What he ate was different; what he wore was different, as were his customs. The Bible says that he prayed three times a day. He was righteous, and his life was a witness for God. In fact, Daniel's enemies couldn't find anything against him. About all they could say was that Daniel was a man "in whom is the Spirit of the Holy God" (Daniel 5:11).

As I continued reading, I found what I believed was the key to Daniel's success in his walk with God. It's in Daniel 10:12: "Do not fear, Daniel, for from the first day that you set your heart to understand, and to humble yourself before God, your words were heard; and I have come because of your words." *Bang!* That's the secret! Daniel did two things every day: (1) he set his heart to understand, and (2) he humbled himself before God.

To understand what? God's will for him each day! Because he prayed so much and spent time connected to God, Daniel was able to understand and know—perhaps even hear God's voice telling him—how to represent Him every day. And then he humbled himself before God.

I remember that when I read this in 1995, I immediately thought back to

1990, the year I was diagnosed with linear scleroderma. I was nineteen years old, had recorded three albums, and was beginning to play in large venues for important people. Things were going well! I figured this was just the beginning and that more success and opportunities would come. Instead of focusing on Jesus, I looked at myself. I became proud and arrogant.

When the linear scleroderma disfigured my face, I lost my self-confidence. I became angry and bitter. And I questioned God. I felt singled out. This was a rare illness. Back in 1990, less than a thousand people had been diagnosed with the general condition of scleroderma (there are variations of it). I remember looking in the mirror, seeing the "ugly" person I had become, and asking God, "Why are You doing this to me?"

I later learned that in nearly 90 percent of the cases of people who have scleroderma, the disease manifests itself systemically, spreading to joints, muscles, and organs all over the body until the person eventually dies. Yet I was in the 10 percent of those in whom the condition stays localized and doesn't spread. This caused me to wonder yet again: *Why me? How come I am not in the other group?* I began to wonder if instead of God *causing* this disease to happen to me, perhaps He *allowed* it to happen so that I could stop looking at myself and look to Him, realizing that He is the Giver of talents and gifts, and the glory should be given to Him. (After all, God never *causes* bad things to happen to His children; this is the job of the devil. God *allows* things to happen for a purpose, which we usually don't understand just yet.)

I had learned this lesson in 1995. Now, seven years later, was this just the natural course of the disease, returning as Dr. Falanga had told me it probably would? Or was the Lord trying to get my attention once again? Was there another lesson to learn? After all, I was once again having a lot of success. Outside the United States, I had performed for governors, mayors, even a head of state. Did I need to be humbled, so that I could stop relying on myself and focus on Christ once again?

The thought that I was becoming puffed up and proud cut me to the heart. I sought the Lord and asked Him to forgive me and use me once again. And I decided that I wanted to do what Daniel did. Every day I would (1) set my heart to understand God's will for me, and (2) humble myself before God.

As I returned to the question of what to do about the linear scleroderma, I vowed that, no matter what the consequence, I would not go back to taking the medications that had harmed me so much the first time around. I was going to look to natural treatments for answers.

CHAPTER 5

FORTE PIANO

{Loud and Accented, Then Immediately Soft}

I n terms of concerts and travel, 2003 was the busiest year I had ever had—182 presentations. Emily and I took our usual vacation at the beginning of 2003 and went to London. But apart from that, we weren't spending much time together. She was busy pursuing her music career in Nashville, and I was working as hard as I could to support her. As a result, we began to drift apart. She wanted and needed me to take time to be with her, but I was busy doing everything I could to support her.

We began to get frustrated, and discord set in. I didn't go to Nashville very often, and when she came home, I was gone or not much in the mood to spend meaningful time together.

Emily had been taking vocal lessons from an excellent coach in Nashville by the name of Chris Beatty, and the results were paying off. She gained strength, control, and clarity; doors were opening up. She signed on with Tri-Star Enter-tainment and eventually got a songwriting deal. Tri-Star was pitching her to re-cord labels, and the artist with whom she appeared on the video was also getting her some opportunities. By the end of 2004, Emily was about to sign a record contract and go into the studio. But at that point, she decided that this industry and career wasn't for her, and she walked away from it all. Her decision cost her a great deal, as her management company required repayment for walking out on her contract. It was a difficult decision, but I am proud of her for leaving that industry behind.

By the middle of 2003, Emily had written a number of fantastic songs, so we decided that she should record a religious album. I asked Paul Tucker—my good friend and someone I had worked with to arrange and produce five albums from 1991 to 1999—to produce Emily's album.

I had now performed a number of times for different functions at LCCA and had become better acquainted with Mr. Preston and Mr. Hunter. Life Care Centers of America had a first-rate recording studio right there in Cleveland, Tennessee. Once upon a time, it was open to the public for rental and use. (I understand that Larnelle Harris loved to record there, and that his arranger and producer did a great deal of work there.) But now, the studio was closed to the public and was mostly used for in-house productions.

When I rang Scott Lingerfelt, a chief engineer, to inquire about the availability of the studio, he told me that it wasn't open to the public. But he thought that if I asked Mr. Hunter, he'd probably let us use it. I called Mr. Hunter's assistant, Kelly Wilcoxson, and after talking with him, she called me back and told me we were welcome to rent the studio for this project. I was thrilled. That meant we didn't have to travel anywhere in order to record the album. Over the course of two weeks, we worked day and night until the project was done. The result was an amazing album.

Emily and Paul worked together beautifully. Paul is one of the best vocal coaches I've ever seen, and Emily was up to the task. She sang with so much conviction; her interpretation was flawless. The songs she wrote fit just right with the others we chose to include. The musicians were fabulous, and the end product turned out to be everything we had hoped for.

Emily didn't travel with me much or promote the album. But we had done a duet, "Unfailing Love," on the album. The arrangement was haunting and melancholy. She sang the melody, and I harmonized and played an obbligato. I played this song at nearly every concert, and people bought it like crazy. Even today, people ask me for that album and wonder if Emily is going to record another one.

In September of 2003, I returned to Australia for the first time in ten years. Linda Hill organized the tour, and I had fourteen presentations in sixteen days. I performed in colleges, churches, and a couple of camp meetings in Queensland and northern New South Wales. One of the churches was called Living Waters in Terrigal. It was a relatively new congregation that met in a school hall. Pastors Barry and Lyn were dynamic, enthusiastic leaders of the church. After the service was over, we were invited to have lunch at the home of Ken and Pam Duncan. Ken is an incredibly gifted panoramic photographer; his photography is known all around the world. We spent a beautiful afternoon with Ken, Pam, and their daughter, Jessica. Since then, we've had the opportunity to get together on a number of occasions. I own some of his breathtaking prints, and one of his photos is the cover of my album *Wonderful Peace,* volume 4 of Simply Classic Hymns.

In November, Emily and I traveled to Anchorage and Sitka, Alaska, for a long weekend of concerts. This was my second visit to this beautiful state, and we saw some of nature's incredible landscapes—rugged mountains, mammoth glaciers, and pristine bodies of water. We had a lovely time in the midst of what were some very difficult times for us. When we went to Spain on vacation in January 2004, we invited one of our good friends, Heide Wilson, to join us on part of the trip. After a concert in Valencia, a young couple, Enoc Diestre and Alba Balué, invited us to go out to eat, and Heide discovered *horchata* milk. She fell in love with it and joked that she wanted to start a business in the United States bottling *horchata* and selling it in volume. After leaving Valencia, we went to Barcelona. I absolutely fell in love with Barcelona, and we packed a week's worth of activities into a short amount of time before coming home.

People ask me if I still enjoy traveling. While I don't much enjoy the process (delayed flights, missed connections, lost bags, etc.), I still have a passion for seeing new and old places, meeting people, making new friends, and seeing old friends.

Posing with Pastor Barry and Ken Duncan before the opening of his new gallery in New South Wales, Autstralia.

CHAPTER 6
GRANDIOSO
{Grandly}

The weekend of April 16–18, 2004, I traveled to New Jersey and New York for a series of concerts. I presented the worship service in the morning at the Robbinsville Seventh-day Adventist Church near Trenton, New Jersey, had a concert at the Fellowship Deaconry in Liberty Corner, New Jersey, that evening, and on Sunday afternoon had another concert at the First Presbyterian Church of Glen Cove, New York.

Monday morning, at the crack of dawn, I flew to Dayton, Ohio, where for three and a half years I had played every month at a network of hospitals. My job was to go around the hospital units and provide music therapy for the patients and staff. The results were absolutely phenomenal—the stress levels of the staff decreased significantly, and the patients' mood changed dramatically. I looked at the heart rate and blood pressure monitors and noticed the numbers ease down as I played.

I had met Fred Manchur, the president of the Kettering Health Network, years before in Bakersfield, California, while he was president of San Joaquin Community Hospital. He invited me one year to play for several hospital functions during December (physicians' banquet, employee banquet, etc.), and one afternoon I suggested I go to some of the patient rooms to play Christmas carols for them. Many of those patients would not be home for Christmas, and some would never get to go home. So Fred grabbed a small boom box, and we began to visit patient rooms.

Later he told me that he had to walk out of the room a couple of times because he was overcome with emotion seeing the joyful response of the patients. He had never forgotten that experience, and sometime after becoming the president of the Kettering Health Network, he invited me to come there and do the same for the entire medical network. It was to be a year-long contract, but somehow it lasted three and a half years. I am thankful to him for the opportunity to reach out to people in such need.

Getting back to April 17, 2004, after the worship service in Trenton, New Jersey, ended, I gathered my things to head to Liberty Corner for the evening presentation at Fellowship Deaconry. The people there are dedicated servants of God, and they have a number of great programs and outreach to the community. Often, I have to travel a significant distance to get from one concert to the next. I prefer, of course, to have the concerts in close proximity to one another, but that doesn't always happen. I've flown all night to get to the next concert; I've driven all night as well and have generally done whatever it takes to make it all happen.

But this weekend was pretty easy: I had only an hour's drive to get to Liberty Corner. I was there by 3:00 P.M. So I headed to the administration office, let the person in charge know I was there, and got the key to my guest room. I was able to go to my room, lie down, rest and relax, and prepare mentally and spiritually for the concert. At 5:25 P.M., I headed to the cafeteria to eat supper. At 6:25 P.M., I got in my rental car to drive to the auditorium to meet with the audio and video engineers, do a sound check, and get ready for the concert that was to begin at 7:30 P.M.

Just as I was about to insert the key into the ignition, a chilling question reverberated in the recesses of my brain: *Where is my violin?* Immediately, I looked in the back seat of my Chevy Impala. I knew the violin wasn't in the trunk because (1) I never store my violin there, and (2) I had already emptied the trunk and taken its contents to the guest room. The unthinkable had happened. I had left my violin on the front pew of the church in Trenton. I had brought *everything* with me from the morning service, *except* my violin!

Fear and panic set in. *What can I do? I don't have time to go back for it. It takes an hour to get there, and the concert begins in an hour!* I rang the pastor of the church on his mobile phone. I had called him a few hours earlier, but this time he didn't answer. So I tried calling him at home. No response. The last number I had was for the church, and when I rang there, nobody picked up.

Now fear and panic turned into shaking and perspiring. My concert was one in a series. People were paying for their tickets. How were they going to react when the person introducing me came onstage and said, "Ladies and gentlemen, welcome to tonight's concert! The violinist is here, without his violin"? What was I going to do? I couldn't sing!

The food I had just eaten began to rumble inside my stomach. I began to despair. Then, all of a sudden, I stopped myself and thought, *Wait a minute. If God has helped me in the past, why can't I ask Him to help me again?* There was no time to lose! So I closed my eyes and prayed, "Dear Lord, You know what's going on here. If there's something You can do to help me get my violin back, please make it quick!"

I stood there for just a moment, catching my breath. And then, the Lord planted a thought in my mind. On my way into the church that morning, I had briefly chatted with a lady whose family I had met before. Several years ago, her husband pastored a church in Medford, Oregon. Before we parted ways, she gave me her family's contact information: address, phone number, and e-mail address. I quickly located the little piece of paper that contained this invaluable information! And I rang her home.

Now, I *needed* her to be home! After two rings, Mrs. Lillian answered. "Hi, Lillian," I said quickly. "This is Jaime Jorge, and I'm desperate!"

"What is going on?" she asked.

I explained my dilemma to her. She said, "Hang on a second. Let me talk with my husband." A few seconds went by that seemed like hours. Then she picked up the phone and began speaking, "Don't worry, Jaime. My husband has a key to the church. If you tell us where you are and how to get there, we'll go to the church, pick up your violin, and bring it to you."

"Thank you!" I responded. And then I yelled inside my head, *Hallelujah!*

By now it was about 6:40 P.M. Lillian and her husband would need to fly low even to get the violin to me around 7:40 P.M. But I figured I could stall until then. I headed over to the auditorium for the sound check. When I arrived, the engineers were waiting for me. I burned the CD with all the tracks, gave them the DVD for the video, and went up on stage. They played the music through the monitor speakers, then the house speakers, and then they tried the DVD. I spoke into the microphone, "One, two, three, testing, testing, one, two, three." At that point, I gave them all the signal cues for anything we needed to adjust once the program began, and I said, "Thank you, gentlemen; we're ready to go."

One of them asked, "Jaime, why don't you take out your violin and play it in front of the mic so we can hear it and equalize it?"

And I shot back, "Because I can tell you guys are so professional that I don't want to take the violin out of the case needlessly until it's time to begin the concert." They must've liked that because they didn't say another word!

At that point, I went to check on the product table, and after that I paced back and forth, waiting for the violin. Of course, nobody knew what was going on. At 7:15 P.M., I went backstage to pray with the pastor and leader of Fellowship Deaconry Christian Conference Center. And at 7:23 P.M., my cell phone rang. It was Lillian. I expected her to tell me that they were just a few minutes away. What she said was, "Jaime, we've had a couple of delays and glitches, and we are just now leaving the church." *What?* It was going to take them an hour to get to me. That would be about the halfway point of the concert! Nobody was going to wait fifty minutes! My heart sank.

I decided I would try to talk to the audience and share my life story until Lillian arrived. I also figured I could buy some precious time by delaying the start of the concert ten or fifteen minutes. So I told the pastor that I needed to go to the restroom. I figured he'd have to wait for me to come out of the restroom before commencing the evening. Boy, was I wrong!

At 7:30 P.M. on the dot, he went up on stage—without me—to start the evening! He was a very exacting timekeeper!

He stood up on the stage, welcomed the audience, thanked them for their presence, had a couple of announcements, prayed to open the concert, and introduced me. The grand total of time I had bought myself? Seven minutes. *Seven minutes!* I was dead in the water, and I knew it. At 7:37 P.M., I went up on the stage, without my violin. The few hundred people in the audience were looking at me as if to say, "Where's your violin?" I opened my mouth even though I had no idea what to say, and this is what came out: "Good evening! I know you're here for a concert, but before I begin playing the violin, I feel impressed to talk to you."

I began to talk. And I talked. And I talked! In fact, I talked for forty-three minutes without stopping! During this time, I told the people the story of my life. I preached every sermon I knew. I remember looking at the clock in the back of the auditorium every few minutes and praying as I spoke, *Lord,* please *send Lillian.* By now it was 8:20 P.M., and I was in the middle of my last story. I simply could not think of another anecdote to share. It was down to the wire. The only thing I could do was to tell the truth about what was going on.

And then all of a sudden, a door opened slowly in the back of the auditorium. Can you imagine the relief I felt when I saw Lillian walk in with my violin? Yippee! Praise God! She made her way to the front of the auditorium, set the violin case down on the front row, and tiptoed to the back once again.

At that point, I was so relieved and elated that I stopped in the middle of that story and announced to the audience, "I'll finish this story later, but right now, I feel impressed to play the violin for you!" Nobody seemed to mind or think anything of it! I walked down to the front row, opened my violin case, took out my violin, attached the shoulder rest to the bottom of the violin, wound up my bow, returned to the stage, and proceeded to play song after song after song without uttering more than a few words here and there the rest of the evening.

When the concert was over and I went to the back to greet the folks, everyone thought this was how the concert was supposed to be—first the testimony and preaching, and then the music! Everyone was happy. Then a gentleman approached the small crowd at the table and said out loud, "Brother Jaime, I noticed at a specific point in the concert that someone came in and brought you your violin." I thought to myself, *This guy has figured out what happened, and he's going to blurt it out in front of everyone present!* I held my breath. Then he continued, "Ever since I saw this, I've wondered, *Does Jaime Jorge have an assistant that carries his violin for him wherever he goes?"*

That was the craziest thing I'd ever heard! If only he knew! I smiled at him, said "No," and continued talking to people.

I'm sure you can imagine the sense of relief and elation I felt as I left the grounds and headed for my hotel that everything had worked out OK. I praised the Lord out loud in the car, thanking Him for His goodness and mercy, for providing a way for me to get my violin back and being able to do the concert.

One of my favorite verses in Scripture is John 15:7: "If you abide in Me, and My words abide in you, you will ask what you desire, and it shall be done for you." Thank You, Jesus! What a beautiful promise. I believe that verse wholeheartedly and want to claim it. We have a very powerful God on our side who is ready and willing to help us. But often we don't have enough faith in Him, or we're not abiding in Him, in order to receive the great blessings He has in store for us.

CHAPTER 7

DOLOROSO

{Sorrowfully; Plaintively}

As Emily and I drifted apart, I looked for distractions that seemed to make me feel better. I had gotten to the point in our marriage where I was frustrated, exasperated, and even angry. I didn't know what to do to fix our relationship, and eventually I just gave up. I think I had a something like a midlife crisis in 2003; I went out and purchased a sports car. I had always dreamed of owning an Acura NSX, and I happened to mention this to someone I knew in the Chattanooga area. He told me his friend owned one and offered to take me to see it and find out if his friend wanted to sell it. So we went to the home of Mickey García, a guy who was originally from Cuba and had a passion for cars. He was a perfusionist, but his love was cars. He owned a small dealership that bought and sold exotic cars. He told me he had personally owned close to thirty cars and enjoyed his hobby tremendously. I was amazed at the thought of having had so many different cars. At that point in my life I had owned a grand total of six cars; my very first one had been a lowly Chevrolet Chevette. But Mickey's cars had been Porsches, Ferraris, and so on.

He told me he wasn't really looking to sell the NSX; but when I told him about my long-standing desire to own one, he agreed to sell it to me. I didn't tell Emily before buying the car, and it made her pretty upset that I had made such a major purchase without even consulting her. I simply told her that since I was the only one in the family who worked and brought home the bacon, I didn't think she had any right to demand that I consult with her about the purchase, much less torpedo it.

About this same time, I also invested in a business and cosigned on the home loan of someone I had known for several years. Obviously, Emily was less than thrilled when I shared with her that I'd done these things—also without consulting her.

It seemed that all we ever did was argue, so instead of coming home to address our issues, I stayed on the road more, did more concerts, and came home less. By that time, our music ministry had grown to the point that I could use part-time help in the office. Instead of having to take care of the day-to-day details—answering calls, sending out orders for products that came in via our Web site, phone, fax, or snail mail, as well as the plethora of details needed to run an office—I was able to hire a fantastic lady, Georgie Dornick, who did so much for me for several years. I could call her at 3:00 A.M. and ask her to put a box of products on a plane by 7:00 A.M., and she would be ready and willing. This happened on more than one occasion when UPS sent a shipment to Texas instead of to Baltimore!

As I looked back at our marriage, I wondered how something so right had gone so wrong. They say that the first year of marriage is the most difficult one. For Emily and me, I think our first year was the best one. We spent so much time together, went so many places, and were so very happy. The second, third, and fourth years were wonderful also. After 2000, Emily began to travel less. Her body was showing signs of fatigue. Her asthma was flaring up again. Traveling made it worse. Being apart was difficult. I sure missed her while I was on the road. Being apart was probably even more difficult for her, because she was at home and lonely. I remember one time I was in Brazil (probably 1998 or 1999), and I called her one night on the phone. She was crying. "Sweetie pie, please come home. I miss you so much." It broke my heart. But I couldn't come home. I couldn't afford to change my ticket.

After a while, those feelings went from sadness to frustration and bitterness. None of our problems were earth-shattering. But we allowed bitterness, frustration, and even anger to set in, and we never recovered. We went to counseling. In fact, we went to four different counselors in the Chattanooga area and met with another via phone. One counselor probably did more harm than good. Emily met with him once or twice before I met with him. By the time we went to see him together, he was convinced that I needed to stop traveling and doing concerts immediately and get a real job. I told him that this wasn't some glamour trip I was on, rather it was a calling to a ministry. I had walked away from medical school before I felt called to be a minister of music. But he had pretty much decided that I was living in a dream world and had to stop the concerts.

As Emily voiced her discontent more and more, I had less desire to listen or work on our problems. I spent less and less time at home, and we communicated less and less. I continued to support her and provide for everything she needed in Nashville, but our relationship was broken.

By the end of the summer of 2003, I had pretty much given up on our marriage. I say that now with regret and pain. Oh how I wish I would have run *to* the Lord instead of *away* from Him. Slowly, my heart turned cold and numb. I figured there was no way to fix things and that the best thing to do was to get a divorce. It didn't help that Emily's manager at Tri-Star Sports and Entertainment was subtly urging her to get a divorce. She'd tell Emily that she would have a lot more appeal and success if she were single.

The years 2003 and 2004 were the two worst years of my life—up to that point. The next three years would be even worse! The sadness, pain, frustration, and anger created a vicious cycle that didn't allow us to change course. It often seemed that I could do nothing right in Emily's eyes, and that she could do nothing right in mine. I was afraid to ask for help, because I didn't want anyone to know that we were having problems. I began to withdraw and became depressed. But at the same time, I hated to be alone. I felt scared and uncomfortable in my own skin. I just wanted road noise—things that took up my time and didn't allow me to think or feel too much.

In June of 2004, we had divorce papers drawn up. We had both pretty much agreed that when I returned from California, I would sign them, and we'd wait for the court date and let it become effective. I had concerts in Central California that weekend, which was the same weekend that President Ronald Reagan was being buried. As I drove along Interstate 5, north of Los Angeles into Bakersfield, the sun was setting. A sense of deep sorrow and despair came over me, and I heard a voice saying, *"Don't give up just yet."* I decided to hang in there and try to work things out. However, that feeling didn't last long.

On November 18, 2004, Emily and I made the trip to the county courthouse where Emily's lawyer had filed for divorce. In Hamilton County (at least back then), all divorce notices were published in the newspaper, and we didn't want people in our home area coming across this bit of information. So we had filed in another county. When we showed up in court that day, the judge asked us if we wanted to go through with the divorce. We said Yes, he signed the papers, and it was over. I didn't fully grasp the gravity of what had just happened. I just felt a certain sense of relief.

Emily stayed in our home until she moved a few months later into her own house. For the rest of 2004 and half of 2005, I didn't want to look back. I made myself extremely busy doing concerts: 203 concerts in 2004 and 2005; 207 in 2006; and I maxed out at 233 concerts in 2007. It was 2010 before I dipped under 200 concerts in a year.

At some point in 2005, I began praying in earnest. I asked God to forgive me for not trusting in Him and for not letting Him be in control of my life. And I told Him that if He wanted to bring Emily and me together again, I was willing to do His will. There's no doubt that the Lord worked in my heart, because all the anger and frustration I harbored were gone. I felt peace and love. I went to talk to Emily in November 2005 to ask her if she was willing to work things out. For most of 2006, we worked to reconcile and come together again.

As I look back, I realize that neither of us was fully surrendered to the Lord. We went back and forth for a couple of years trying to work things out, but we only hurt ourselves and each other in the process. The pain was overwhelming. I remember nights when I would cry until I threw up. I was all alone in my house, and I was afraid. Some days, I didn't even come out of my bedroom. I couldn't sleep at night. I wanted to stop doing concerts. I felt so empty. During one of these stretches of depression, I dropped from 198 pounds to 157 pounds. One time I counted how many days I'd gone without eating: eight. I became so skinny, people would come up before or after concerts and ask me if I were sick. Someone once even asked me if I had AIDS.

When I stood in front of people, I felt as if they could see the nakedness in my heart and soul. I felt completely uncovered, insecure, and unprepared. I didn't think God could use me anymore. So I began to think about putting down my violin forever and walking away from the music ministry God had called me to.

One time I was in Oregon. It was one of those weekends with several concerts. On this particular morning, the service was about to begin. The worship leaders were waiting for me to pray with them before going onto the platform. But I was in the bathroom crying. *What am I going to say to the congregation? What a loser! I am such a fake!*

Then I heard a still, small Voice: *"Go and share your story, Jaime. It's not about how talented, prepared, or confident you are. It's all about My grace. My love. My Son, Jesus Christ."*

I wiped away my tears and prayed with those who were waiting for me. As I stepped out in front of the congregation, I shared my music and the story of what God was doing in my life. And I watched His Spirit at work. Several people accepted salvation. Others recommitted their lives and sought a closer walk with God. But no one there could imagine how much my own life had been changed by Jesus Christ—only a few moments beforehand.

I understood my responsibility in letting my marriage fall apart. I stopped making excuses or blaming Emily. My marriage was over forever. I had lost my sweetie pie. The voice that made me weak in the knees when she sang was silenced. A mutual friend from British Columbia, Rita Corbett, called Emily my "songbird." Indeed, my songbird was gone. But it didn't mean God couldn't forgive me, heal me, or use me. It was the beginning of a long journey back to God, a journey that would teach me once again to rely on Him and not on my own perceived strength, knowledge, or abilities. A journey that would teach me humility, once again.

CHAPTER 8

TREMOLO

{Shaking; Rapidly Moving the Bow While the Arm Is Tense}

One of the greatest and most important qualities a human being can have is humility. Both my parents always inculcated in me a sense of humility. My mother would remind me that just because I had a gift from God didn't mean I should show off, much less look down on people that don't seem to have as much musical talent. My dad gave me some biblical perspective. He'd point out Proverbs 16:18: "Pride goes before destruction, and a haughty spirit before a fall." He explained to me that Lucifer's downfall was pride. Lucifer wanted to be like God and rebelled. As I say in concert sometimes, "Pride turned Lucifer into Satan." Ezekiel 28:17 says, "Your heart was lifted up [became proud] because of your beauty; you corrupted your wisdom for the sake of your splendor."

As I read and studied the Scriptures, I saw how destructive pride is. It brought down many people. Haman, in the story of Esther, ultimately lost his life because of it.

> Then Haman told them of his great riches, the multitude of his children, everything in which the king had promoted him, and how he had advanced him above the officials and servants of the king.
>
> Moreover Haman said, "Besides, Queen Esther invited no one but me to come in with the king to the banquet that she prepared; and tomorrow I am again invited by her, along with the king. Yet all this avails me nothing, so long as I see Mordecai the Jew sitting at the king's gate" (Esther 5:11–13).

Mordecai would not bow down to Haman, and it made Haman so angry he tried to destroy Mordecai and the Jews. The plot was ultimately brought to the knowledge of the king, and Haman paid the price with his life.

Why do you think the powerful and mighty king, Nebuchadnezzar, was humbled to the point of eating grass like an animal and dwelling with the cattle for some time? You guessed it—pride!

> The king spoke, saying, "Is not this great Babylon, that I have built for a royal dwelling by my mighty power and for the honor of my majesty?"
>
> While the word was still in the king's mouth, a voice fell from heaven: "King Nebuchadnezzar, to you it is spoken: the kingdom has departed from you! And they shall drive you from men, and your dwelling shall be with the beasts of the field. They shall make you eat grass like oxen; and seven times shall pass over you, until you know that the Most High rules in the kingdom of men, and gives it to whomever He chooses" (Daniel 4:30–32).

I would like to share just two more experiences from the Bible that address the dangerous condition and sin of pride. The first one is found in 2 Kings 18:17–19:37. Sennacherib, the king of Assyria, was a very powerful, rich, and feared ruler. He had conquered many nations around him, and he decided to attack Jerusalem and the people of Israel. So he sent the Tartan (probably meaning "commander in chief"), the Rabsaris (probably meaning "chief officer"), and the Rabshakeh (probably meaning "chief of staff") to convince King Hezekiah and the people of Israel to pay tribute to Assyria and come under his rulership (see 2 Kings 18:17).

Eliakim, Shebna, and Joah, representing King Hezekiah, listened as the Rabshakeh pompously delivered to them the words of the Assyrian king: "Where are the gods of Hamath and Arpad? Where are the gods of Sepharvaim and Hena and Ivah? Indeed, have they delivered Samaria from my hand? Who among all the gods of the lands have delivered their countries from my hand, that the LORD should deliver Jerusalem from my hand?" (2 Kings 18:34, 35). King Sennacherib was a haughty and proud man.

Sennacherib also sent messengers to King Hezekiah, with a letter repeating his proud demands. Hezekiah went up to the house of the Lord, opened the letter before Him, and prayed (see 2 Kings 19:14, 15). And the response from God was utterly definitive: "And it came to pass on a certain night that the angel of the LORD went out, and killed in the camp of the Assyrians one hundred and eighty-five thousand; and when people arose early in the morning, there were the corpses—all dead. So Sennacherib king of Assyria departed and went away, returned home, and remained at Nineveh. Now it came to pass, as he was worshiping in the temple of Nisroch his god, that his sons Adrammelech and Sharezer struck him down with the sword; and they escaped into the land of Ararat" (verses 35–37).

Nearly two hundred thousand soldiers in the army of Sennacherib were killed in one night! And not long after that, the proud king was killed by his own sons.

The second and last story I want to share with you is found in Acts 12:21–23. This is truly a jaw-dropping story. "So on a set day Herod, arrayed in royal apparel, sat on his throne and gave an oration to them [the people of Tyre and Sidon]. And the people kept shouting, 'The voice of a god, and not of a man!' Then immediately an angel of the Lord struck him [Herod], because he did not give glory to God. And he was eaten by worms and died."

As these stories make clear, pride is a very dangerous sin. God hates pride, because it tends to put us above Him. Proverbs 6:16, 17 says, "These six things the LORD hates, yes, seven are an abomination to Him: a proud look . . ." Pride is at the top of the list of things God hates!

When you stand up in front of people, whether to speak, to preach, to sing, or to play, it is easy to become proud when you receive accolades and compliments. I know, because it has happened to me many times. It's so easy to start to think, *I'm pretty good. Everything being said about me is true; I'm awesome.* I am very thankful that the Lord has gotten my attention frequently, in order to remind me not to look at myself, but to look at Him.

Once while I was performing in a large church, I was wearing a black suit and a white shirt. I was feeling pretty good about myself, when I realized (thanks to people close to the front who kept pointing at my pants) that my zipper was open!

Another time, I was skipping up the steps to the stage, showing off my "athletic" abilities, when I tripped. Trying to avoid falling on my face (or worse, landing on my violin or breaking it), I took a pretty big leap with the foot that hadn't tripped. The only problem was that my pants tore in front from the bottom of the crotch to the back just below the belt. So for most of the concert I had to stand with my heels and ankles touching and take baby steps any time I wanted to walk around so that the entire audience hopefully would not see the obvious, glaring fact that my pants were completely ripped down the middle.

A couple of years ago, I was invited to go to Southern California to do several benefit concerts for Christian schools and academies. Having attended Christian schools of different denominations myself, I believe in Christian education! So I happily accepted the invitation. I decided to wear a "snazzy" suit I hadn't worn in a while. I went out and bought some sweet shirts and ties so I'd have new accessories for this tour. When I went to put my suit on, everything fit just right—except my pants. I had gained so much weight that the zipper went up only three-fourths of the way. It was so obvious that not even the belt could hide the space at the top where the pants would button. So I had to commit another fashion faux pas, which was to button all three of the buttons on my jacket, and on top of that I had to hold my breath, hoping my pants wouldn't fall down in the middle of the concert!

In June 2011, I was invited by a new friend, Mario Peralta, to come to his state of Tabasco, Mexico, and put on some concerts for the community on behalf of the state government. As a young state congressman, he had a lot of energy and enthusiasm to implement many positive programs to improve the communities of his state. We went to several colleges and universities to put on concerts that would encourage and inspire the young people. On this particular day, I had a presentation in the middle of the morning at the Tecnológico de Comalcalco, a technological college in the city of Comalcalco. Now I have been to Mexico at least fifty times in the last twenty years, and I have the misfortune of often, if not always, falling under the inauspicious effects of Montezuma's revenge.

That morning, as Mario and I finished breakfast in Villahermosa and headed to Comalcalco, I felt my stomach begin to churn. I always travel with activated charcoal pills when going overseas, and that's saved me many times. But the bottle of pills was in my hotel room, and I didn't want to go back. I figured I'd be OK by the time we arrived at the Tecnológico. Boy, was I wrong! We arrived there, and I should've headed straight for the bathroom. But since we were running a bit late and I wanted to put on a stoic face, I tried to ignore it.

As the concert progressed, my stomach grew worse and worse. I got to the point that I didn't think I was going to make it to the end. I tried everything I could—mind over matter, not thinking about it, praying, and moving and shaking my body even more than I normally do when I play. I was perspiring profusely because I was in so much discomfort. When I finished the last song, the "Hallelujah Chorus," people began to stand for a very generous ovation. The dean of the college came up to present me with a special recognition consisting of oratory and a plaque. Unfortunately, I was not going to be able to stick around for any of it. As soon as I put my violin down, I made a beeline for the back of the auditorium, and then I ran to the bathroom.

Unfortunately, in many (if not, most) bathrooms in Mexico, tissue paper is *not* provided. You must bring your own. So I had to wait until someone put two and two together and followed me to the bathroom, at which time I was able to make an embarrassing request for tissue paper. I was probably there for twenty-five minutes!

Sometimes through funny experiences like these and through others much more serious—such as the linear scleroderma condition I have—God has allowed me to be humbled. I'm very thankful for the fact that God loves us all so much that He corrects us in order to save us from ourselves. I love the passage in Proverbs 3:11, 12: "My son, do not despise the chastening of the Lord, nor detest His correction; for whom the Lord loves He corrects." So when people come to share with me their heartfelt appreciation and compliments for blessing them, I desire to always say, "Praise God!" Because He is the One who gave me the talent to play.

I am also learning to pray for others who have yet to learn much about humility. It's one thing if you don't claim to do what you do for God's honor and glory.

There is a great contemporary violinist whom I admire very much as a musician. But I've heard firsthand experiences from people who've met him that he is an extremely arrogant and haughty individual. But it's quite another thing when you're supposed to be singing, playing, speaking, painting, or preaching for the Lord.

It was July 2005, and I was about to perform on one of the biggest stages of my life. In terms of numbers, it *was* the biggest stage; there were sixty thousand people present on the closing night of the General Conference Session at the Edward Jones Dome in St. Louis, Missouri. I was the third of four musicians performing for the Parade of Nations program. All four of us had to be backstage, ready to be called to share our talents. The house band, led by my friend John Stoddart was playing beautifully.

With sixty thousand people cheering and singing, I could hardly hear myself think, even backstage. But there was one performer who had his cell phone attached to his ear the entire time, as if he were on the phone talking with others. Clearly, it was a Do Not Disturb sign. I had been on the same program with this individual before and I would have simply greeted him, but I wasn't about to bother him then. When it was my turn, I was taken to the right side of the stage, to be ready to walk on to the center of the stage to share the hymn "Face to Face."

I was able to glance at and greet some of the other band members. One of them was a fabulous guitarist by the name of Roland Gresham. I hadn't seen him in eighteen years! By that point, as we were getting close to the end, the cell-phone-carrying musician was seated close to the band but away from the center stage lights. At some point, stage personnel took me over to my spot, set up my microphone, and I waited for the lights to go on, the band to start, and to begin playing my special number. I don't remember much of the performance itself. With so many tens of thousands of people there, many of them singing along, it was an incredible adrenaline rush. About all I remember is that as I walked off the stage, my shirt was soaking wet under my suit jacket.

As the program continued and the music shifted, I walked toward the band and toward the stage exit. The musician with the cell phone had stopped talking on it, and as I walked by him, he extended his arm and said, "Hi, I'm [so and so]." It was as if he were giving me his seal of approval for having performed and now I could address him. I smiled politely, shook his hand, walked right past him, opened my arms, and said to John, who was sitting at the piano just a few feet away, "John, you were awesome, as usual! What an honor to know you."

The other musician probably didn't appreciate the fact that I didn't show him some respect once he had greeted me after I finished performing.

In 2011, La Voz de la Esperanza, the organization I had worked with for nearly twelve years, put on an evangelistic-type program at the revered Lincoln Center in New York City. This was a historic opportunity to share Jesus Christ from a venue that typically hosts classical and secular events. Dr. Frank González's messages were Spirit-filled and stirring, and more than a thousand souls accepted salvation and were baptized during the four-night series.

Of course, music played a central part in this event, and the team of musicians from La Voz as well as other excellent musicians participated, including the powerful vocalist Junior Kelly Marchena; the gifted actor, singer, and TV host Clifton Davis; and my friend and piano virtuoso, Sam Ocampo, to name most of them.

There was another singer who had been scheduled to sing. He's had a long and successful career in contemporary Christian music, and his music is well known and loved around the world. I had met him a few years before when my buddy, Trent DeLong, got married in Arkansas at the Hot Springs Baptist Church. Trent and this musician are friends, and the musician sang at Trent's wedding. It so happens that the musician and I have another mutual friend, who is a physician.

Figuring that this musician would be glad to hear a familiar name, I wanted to share this fact with him. During a break in the wedding rehearsal, I sat behind him and said, "We have a mutual friend, Dr. [so and so]." Now if someone told me that a good friend of mine was also a good friend of his, I'd immediately show some enthusiasm. Instead, this person simply said, "Oh, yeah?" I waited for another word, but he never said anything else, much less turned around to acknowledge me.

It wasn't a big deal, really. But I pray I never treat others with disinterest, no matter how "big" or "little" they may be.

During a very successful evangelistic effort that La Voz de la Esperanza presented at the Poliforum in Tuxtla Gutierrez, Chiapas, Mexico, this same musician also came to perform. Most of the artists hung out in the dressing room. We were all staying in the same hotel too. But this particular musician kept to himself and maintained a distance from all the other participants.

Back to the Lincoln Center. Thousands of people had registered to attend, the place was going to be sold out, even though we weren't selling tickets, and the excitement was palpable. The first meeting was Wednesday night, August 31, and the last one was Saturday night, September 4.

I didn't arrive on the thirty-first as planned because Hurricane Irene wreaked havoc on the region, and my flight from São Paulo, Brazil, like hundreds, if not thousands, of flights was canceled. But upon arriving on September 1, I learned that this musician had botched up his performance on opening night. His pianist changed the key in the middle of a song, and he didn't go up with the pianist. So needless to say, it was not a very good experience. The audience was sorely disappointed, and the song could not be used for the TV broadcast.

In contrast, when we had our twenty-fifth anniversary concert and recording in November 2012, one of the artists we invited was Michael Card. As we worked with his team, it was so easy and seamless to work out all the details. Michael didn't send a fifty-page rider with all kinds of crazy demands. He didn't bring an entourage to look after him. He drove himself to the venue, was helpful, kind, accommodating, and an all-around pleasure to work with that day. As much success as he's had being one of the most prolific songwriters in contemporary Christian music, he is extremely humble and down to earth.

One last story I want to share with you. It is said that the successful actor Telly Savalas, protagonist of the popular TV show *Kojak,* was on a plane once headed to the country of Greece. Sitting next to him in first class was a gentleman who, as the long flight neared Athens, leaned over and said to Mr. Savalas, "Sir, my daughter is a huge fan of yours. Would you mind giving me your autograph so I can surprise her with it?" Mr. Savalas brushed off the man, telling him that he didn't give autographs during vacation.

Once the airplane landed, it headed for the gate. But before it got there, it made a surprise stop in a remote location. The door of the jumbo jet opened, and the gentleman next to Mr. Savalas got up. Someone gathered his carry-on bags for him, and he departed the plane. The door closed, and then the plane headed for the gate. As the plane was taxiing to the gate, Mr. Savalas asked one of the flight attendants, "Who was that guy?"

She responded, "Sir, he's the king of Greece."

Oops!

It is so much better and easier to be humble and to stay humble! If I ever respond to someone or say something in an arrogant manner, you have my permission to call me on it, and remind me that "pride goes before a fall" and that as a servant of God, I don't have the right to treat anyone improperly!

CHAPTER 9
SEMPRE MAESTOSO
{Always Majestically; In a Stately Fashion}

O ne of the greatest joys and honors I've had is to work alongside Dr. Frank González, his wife, Evelyn, and the rest of the La Voz de la Esperanza team. (Some of the team members that I had the pleasure of working alongside with are Orlando Contreras, Edna Zayas, Rita Díaz, "Sir" Charles García, and singing sensation, Junior Kelly Marchena.) At different times and locations, I have spent time with some or all of these fine folks in some of the most exciting and challenging circumstances and places. The single focus for all of us was always to bring souls to Jesus Christ.

I saw God work miracles that strengthened and increased my faith and gave me boldness to think, dream, and act even bigger for God's honor and glory. Let me share some of these stories with you.

In 2003–2004, the Lord impressed Dr. Frank that La Voz de la Esperanza should not only have a radio program but also a TV program. Of course, production costs for TV are much, much higher than they are for radio. So Dr. Frank tried to dismiss this impression, reasoning that the organization couldn't afford it. But God is not to be reasoned away! And so Frank says he got to the point where he couldn't sleep very well because the Holy Spirit wouldn't leave him alone.

So by faith, Frank decided to launch a TV program. The idea was to hold an evangelistic effort in the heart of East Los Angeles, invite the predominantly Hispanic community, present the gospel of Jesus and His love, and record these programs and turn them into a TV series. And of course, we didn't have the hundred thousand dollars needed to record and produce this series.

But as I've learned time and time again, when God is in a thing, it cannot fail. He will provide. It's easy to walk when we see a block of concrete in front of us. But we can see God's power and might much better when we step out into an abyss. This is what happened! We were three months away from the launch of this effort and production, and still there was no money to carry it out.

I was in Washington for a weekend of concerts in June; and as I shared the message through the Word, testimony, and music that morning for the worship service, I felt impressed to share with the congregation our plans for the up-coming evangelistic effort and TV program taping. I usually concentrate on certain mission projects, quite often the work La Voz was doing in Cuba. But that morning, in addition to talking about the work in Cuba, I also mentioned this daunting, upcoming project. As I went to the back of the church to greet people, a gentleman came up to me and asked, "How much money do you need for this project in Cuba?"

I told him, "Twenty-five thousand dollars."

Without hesitating, he responded, "I'll send you twenty-five thousand dollars."

Wow, I thought. *Praise the Lord! These funds will be able to purchase many Bibles and other vital resources!*

From Washington, I traveled to California and then to Cuba. My trips to Cuba had to be coordinated well in advance. First of all, because of the embargo I couldn't just travel to Cuba if I felt like it. It was illegal. The United States government did grant religious and humanitarian organizations a special license to travel to Cuba. But this license was granted only after a rigorous screening and investi-gative process, and it was only good for two years. The most minute details had to be provided when filling out the application in order to receive this two-year license. For example, the application had to include names, addresses, and other information on all the people who would be traveling to Cuba under this license; how long each individual would stay in Cuba; where; and what specific activities they would be carrying out relating to the organization, and so on. Our manager and treasurer would compile all this information and submit the application.

For me, it had to be a Flash Gordon type of trip every time I went. The min-istry and lifeline of our work were the concerts I put on every weekend. You don't go to Cuba to make money. You go to take funds and resources to continue God's work. So I'd finish a weekend of concerts (for me, a typical weekend of concerts has anywhere from three to five concerts beginning Friday evening and ending Sunday night), fly to Cuba, arrive very late Monday night, be there Tuesday through Thurs-day, and return to the United States on Thursday night or Friday early enough to make my concerts for that weekend. During my time in Cuba, I would be visiting churches, seminaries, home churches, pastors, lay missionaries, and so on, taking pictures and gathering stories. Then I would bring back reports to those who had so generously, and sometimes sacrificially, given to further God's work there.

So this time I returned from Cuba to Minnesota for concerts. When I arrived in the United States, I had three voice mail messages from Rita Díaz who is in charge of documenting and processing all the donations that come in to La Voz. Her voice had a vibe of urgency: "Jaime, please call me as soon as you can."

Well, after hearing this three times, I was a bit worried. When I rang her, she told me what had happened. The gentleman that had promised me twenty-five thousand dollars had sent his donation. But instead of sending twenty-five thousand dollars, he sent thirty-five thousand dollars. I was stunned, and I rejoiced, of course. But that wasn't the end of it. He had sent another check. When I called him, he told me what had happened. He went home and prayed. He felt impressed to give more than the amount he had promised, thus the thirty-five thousand dollar check. But then he said that the Holy Spirit impressed him to give a donation for the evangelistic effort and TV taping just over three months away. The amount of the check? You guessed it: one hundred thousand dollars! The exact amount we needed to produce the campaign and the taping. I had tears in my eyes as I spoke with Frank, as he did also when he gathered the La Voz staff to share with them how the Lord was providing!

When the last night of the meetings in Los Angeles came to a close, after hundreds of people had made decisions to accept salvation, we shared with the audience the miracle of this donation. People were moved. We made an appeal for the audience to help us put the programs on TV now that we had been able to record them. We were challenged and amazed when just over one hundred thousand dollars in donations and pledges were received that night! If you're familiar with the demographics of the heart of East Los Angeles and the financial challenges that this community faces, it makes it all the more amazing that these faithful brothers and sisters gave what they had (and, perhaps, what they didn't have) for the Lord's work, after seeing the transforming power of Jesus Christ, through the work of La Voz.

In December 2005, the Lord provided yet again for the mission projects and work of La Voz de la Esperanza. I had spoken to a gentleman who was considering making a contribution but who wasn't quite sure which ministry and what project he should donate to. After sharing with him some of the projects we were planning, I suggested he speak with Frank directly, so that they could talk about vision, mission, and so forth.

It was after Christmas, and I was home for a few days, having concluded my typical, crazy Christmas concert tour. I had waited until this time to have some surgery I needed and was still wobbly from the medication when I received an e-mail from this gentleman. His e-mail said that he had felt impressed to make a four hundred thousand dollar contribution! Before I did anything, I had to make sure the medication wasn't playing tricks with my eyes or mind. I read and reread his e-mail. I was not dreaming. A few days later, I received another e-mail from the same gentleman telling me that he wasn't comfortable with what he'd done. So he was sending *another* four hundred thousand dollar contribution!

Can you imagine the reaction of the staff? Of course we rejoiced and praised the Lord! This money wasn't ours. It was the Lord's, and we would use it as directed to bring light and hope to people. But we were learning that God does not know the meaning of the word *impossible*. And we were learning to trust in Him more. I was also realizing and deciding that I never wanted my lack of faith to be the reason God didn't bless more abundantly!

In mid-April 2006, the very day the team was headed to Houston for the next taping of the *La Voz* TV programs, Rita received a check for fifty thousand dollars. By now, she was becoming accustomed to these mini–heart attacks for the glory of God!

Matthew 7:7 says, "Ask, and it will be given to you." Let us be bold for God. Let us ask Him to do great things for His honor and glory, and He will!

In 2008, state government officials were contacted in order to secure an ideal location for the evangelistic meetings in Chiapas, Mexico—the Poliforum in the capital city Tuxtla Gutiérrez. We were told that it would cost nine thousand dollars per night to rent the facility. We wanted the place for nine nights. Imagine: it would cost eighty-one thousand dollars just to rent the place. Impossible! Dr. Frank, the team, and many others began to pray. They requested an audience with the governor, the Honorable Juan Sabines, hoping to receive a substantial discount. When the meeting began, the governor inquired what group was putting on the event. *"La Voz de La Esperanza,"* we told him. His attention suddenly shifted. It turned out he had listened to the radio broadcast of *La Voz* on Sundays as a boy, and he remembered and loved the programs. He announced that there would be *no charge at all* for the nine nights at the auditorium! Hallelujah! God had once again provided!

Over and over again, I have seen with my own eyes hundreds and thousands of people accept the gift of salvation at the evangelistic campaigns Dr. Frank and La Voz de la Esperanza have put on. I was present at the following events: In 2001 in Cuba, more than 7,000 souls came to Christ. In 2008, again in Cuba, more than 5,100; more than 6,000 through the satellite effort based out of Cochabamba, Bolivia; and more than 3,200 in Chiapas, Mexico. In 2009, more than 350 at the Crystal Cathedral in Garden Grove, California; and in 2011, more than 1,000 at the Lincoln Center in New York City. None of this would have been possible without (1) the blessing and outpouring of the Holy Spirit, (2) the unity and dedication demonstrated by the clergy and laity, and (3) the faithful support of the many donors of La Voz de la Esperanza.

The campaigns in California and New York reinforced my belief that bountiful harvests of souls can happen in the United States. We often went overseas, because that's where we were invited. Sadly, there are still pastors and leaders who are afraid, or perhaps a little jealous, of other pastors who work incessantly at preaching the gospel and who have a burning passion for God. I sometimes sat in on meetings where fields were closed to Dr. Frank and La Voz because some individuals didn't want great results to overshadow them. It should never be about that at all! We should all work together to further God's kingdom. The credit goes to God—not Dr. Frank or any man. I remember one time we met with several pastors from the East Coast about holding a special evangelistic event in that area. One pastor put forth every imaginable obstacle in order to prevent this from happening: a ribbon-cutting ceremony one month, a retreat another, a prayer conference after that, and so on. I shook my head in disbelief at the lack of desire to win souls. No time to preach the gospel? He got angry when I tried to bring this to light during the meeting, and he came to talk to me afterward. I simply told him that my desire was to win souls and that I didn't care about politics or about anyone receiving the credit other than God.

When we were invited to put on evangelistic meetings at the Crystal Cathedral, a local leader, Pastor Alberto Ingleton, brought all the pastors together, and everyone worked together as a cohesive team to maximize their energies, resources, and talents. For the meetings at the Lincoln Center, a local leader, Pastor Michael Guerrero, also led the pastors and church members to create a powerful team that focused on the single goal of having one heart and mind to allow the Holy Spirit to work powerfully. The results spoke for themselves! When, as God's children, we allow Him to take away ego, insecurity, and selfish motives, God will be able to do even greater things for His kingdom and for the eternal gain of many souls. I once heard a preacher say something that shook me to the core: "Jesus didn't come to this world to get us out of hell. He came to get the hell out of *us*." Often I am my own worst enemy. I need to get out of the way and allow God to be in complete control of my life. When that happens, He can do great things!

After seventeen years of leading La Voz de la Esperanza to exponential and explosive growth, Dr. Frank announced his departure to return to the parish ministry. God had accomplished incredible and miraculous things using Dr. Frank and La Voz: historic evangelistic efforts in historic venues; outside-the-box thinking for reaching souls; a seemingly impossible TV program on mainstream, Spanish-language TV; and tens of thousands of souls won for Christ. The constant travel and the pressures of leading a faith ministry can wear on anyone. Health challenges also exacerbated the wear and tear on his body. Besides, Dr. Frank loves pastoral ministry. So when he received a call to pastor in central Florida, he brought it before the Lord. It was evident this was the Lord leading, and he accepted the call. There's no doubt in my mind that Pastor Frank will turn central Florida upside down for the glory of God!

I am going to miss our conversations in buses, cars, and airplanes on the way to or from great events where God's Spirit has clearly been at work in a powerful way. Dr. Frank is one of the most intelligent people I've ever been around, and we have had many a great discussion about theology, history, politics, art, philosophy, and so much more. Dr. Frank is a great leader and I have learned so much from him. But I'm looking forward to visiting with him when I'm passing through Florida or when our paths cross elsewhere. Besides that, I'll continue to be in touch with his family, as his wife, Evelyn, is my booking agent, and his oldest son, Sergio, is one of my best friends.

When Dr. Frank invited me to be a part of La Voz, I immediately began to look down the road. I knew a day would come when he would leave, and I decided I would probably leave with him. So when he made his announcement in 2012, I took a bit of time to think about it and especially to pray. I felt it was time for me to move on as well. I loved the ten-plus years I spent as a part of this organization, and I enjoyed nearly every aspect of what I did: meeting with people, sharing with them about the work this organization was doing, praying with them, supporting mission projects and events around the world, introducing Jesus to many people, soliciting contributions from individuals, spending time with the team, and so forth.

The one thing I never liked, however, was the politics. The La Voz team was, and is, small, so there were never any political issues there. Frank let me do my job without micromanaging me, and I did it with passion and dedication. The results speak for themselves. But there were overlapping layers of organizational oversight that also had a role in the work of La Voz. And sometimes the regulations, procedures, and policies that came out of the discussions at these levels seemed to hinder more than they helped. We hoped that the organizational leaders would understand our simple mission and give us wings to fly. La Voz's only mission is to preach the gospel and win souls for Christ.

Around 2005, I began to realize that the politics involved and the conflicts of interest among some who had oversight of La Voz were causing the ministry to suffer. The chairman of the executive committee once talked to me about a video he had seen on YouTube of a concert I had given at a church where the pastor and local leaders had laid hands on me and prayed. This leader didn't want me to go back there again. Now, I go to all kinds of churches of all kinds of denominations. My job is to share Christ, not to make changes to the way a church does things. And unless it's a principle or a moral issue, I go along with the way that church does things. I've even been to a church where the pastor asked me not to make an appeal for people to accept Christ at the end of the concert. That blew me away because isn't that what a church service is about—introducing people to Jesus and inviting them to accept His gift of salvation? Accepting Jesus as Savior is a central theme of any and all of my presentations. So while I didn't make an altar call or appeal as this pastor requested, the Holy Spirit figured out a way for me to still make an invitation.

But the encumbrances of politics weren't what led me to depart La Voz.

I always felt that when Frank left, I'd leave too. And the other reason for my decision was that, by God's grace, my music ministry had grown tremendously during the last twenty-five years, and I felt the Lord calling me to have a greater role in supporting any and all churches and Christ-centered organizations that would invite our music ministry to provide musical and spiritual presentations, request help raising funds for a project, help out with getting a local music program off the ground, and so on. And so God led me to found a charitable organization called Healing Music, Inc., that I'll discuss later on. But already the dreams are big, and the enthusiasm is high to do great things through this organization.

There were many wonderful, dedicated individuals that served on the executive committee of La Voz and inspired me a great deal. My longtime friend Dr. Steve Peterson supported La Voz with not only his contributions but also with his time. He traveled to Cuba several times to participate in the Caravans of Hope evangelistic programs and missionary endeavors. His soprano saxophone praised the Lord and blessed many in Cuba, Mexico, and in the United States. Sometimes he'd be in surgery all day and most of the night, yet he drove hours and/or flew the next morning to attend the executive committee meetings. I am blessed to count Dr. Steve as my friend!

Someone else that I appreciate, respect, and admire a great deal is Pastor Velino Salazar. He had a passion for promoting and supporting La Voz. He was a tireless defender of the ministry and often opened many doors for La Voz. And he wasn't there just to lend his experience and expertise. He was a faithful contributor. He is also a man of integrity. Many pastors who are invited to speak at other churches receive an honorarium at the end of the day. I'm not saying there's anything wrong with that. I guess that's up to each individual. But I was impressed that when a church representative would come up to Pastor Velino to hand him a check, he'd say, "Thank you so much, but I already receive a salary as a minister of the gospel. I'll accept a fruit basket, a necktie, or something similar, but not a check." That blew me away, frankly. Many times, Pastor Velino and his wife, Esther, opened their home to me and took time to talk to me, pray with me, and encourage me. What a blessing and inspiration they are in my life!

Though we are all humans and make mistakes, when God is in control of our lives, great things can be accomplished for His kingdom, honor, and glory. God used Dr. Frank in a powerful way during the years he led La Voz. He will continue to use him wherever he goes. God wants to use each of us to reach people for Christ!

Dr. Frank González preaching powerfully at the Lincoln Center.

CHAPTER 10
RITARDANDO
{Slowing Down; Decelerating}

P eople often ask me if I love to travel. I can understand why travel might seem like an enticing, glamorous activity. But there is very little that is enticing to me about travel—especially by air. As expansive as the skies are, our air-traffic-control system is antiquated and in desperate need of modernizing. The result is that flights are often delayed. The airlines blame the government; the government blames the airlines; and passengers are tense, frustrated, and angry.

Having said all that, I consider myself very fortunate. Being a frequent flyer with American Airlines, I have been blessed to receive some of the best service and help any passenger could ever hope for. In 1988, when I began flying on a regular basis, there were, and still are, two major airlines flying in and out of Chicago's O'Hare International Airport, the city where my family lived.

United Airlines is actually based in Chicago, and I tried it first. For whatever reason, the treatment I received from United was completely unsatisfactory. So I tried American Airlines, and the rest is history. By the end of 2013, I will likely have flown six million miles on American Airlines. Over the years, I have been the recipient of kindness and beyond-the-call-of-duty service from countless dedicated airline employees. I am even privileged to call some of them my friends.

When I began flying out of Chicago in 1988, there was a particular agent who seemed to be permanently stationed at the first-class and frequent-flier check-in counter. This person always had a smile on her face and was ready to assist every passenger. Cheryl Magnuson was a favorite of the seasoned traveler. Over the course of time, she and I became good friends. That friendship has lasted all of these years. She attended my wedding in 1997 and has been to a concert or two of mine. Every time I fly through O'Hare, I make it a point to find her if she's working, to say "Hi," and exchange a hug.

Norman Hull is another American Airlines agent I became friends with. Every time I call the frequent-flyer desk, I speak to a different agent. But over the course of a few weeks in 1997, I seemed to always talk to the same agent—Norman. As it turned out, he was based in the Raleigh, North Carolina, office, and I was living in Shelby, North Carolina, at the time. And so we began to stay in touch. Norman and his wife attended a concert, and we have remained friends over the years.

When Emily and I moved to Tennessee in 2000, I began flying mostly out of Chattanooga. Even though it has a very small airport, Chattanooga is fairly close to three other airports: Knoxville, Nashville, and Atlanta, Georgia. When flight schedules are more advantageous, I will fly in or out of any of these three other airports. But the best crew of airline agents is in Chattanooga. Agents Jerry, Steve, Shannon, David, Alan, and others take great care of the passengers and make the process of flying, at least in and out of Chattanooga, much more comfortable!

I have also gotten to know several of the hard-working Transportation Security Adminstration (TSA) agents that serve at the Chattanooga airport. Officers John, Laura, Julie, Trishia, Jermaine, and many others carry out their responsibilities in unparalleled fashion, serving both our country and the passengers.

In July 2011, I flew to Montana for four concerts over a weekend. Montana is a huge and beautiful state. But in order to get to the different cities, there is a lot of driving to do. From Friday night to Sunday night, I had presentations in Billings, Bozeman, Kalispell, and Butte.

I flew into Bozeman on Thursday night, because that city would be the most central location for all my travels and concerts. I am pretty sure getting to Bozeman required three flights and two airlines! When I went to collect my bags, they had not made the last flight. This meant that I wouldn't be able to work out the next morning and that I would need to purchase a toothbrush, toothpaste, and other toiletries to use until my bags arrived. But my greater concern was the fact that I had a concert in Billings the next evening and the next flight on Alaska Airlines and Horizon Air would not arrive in Bozeman until late Friday afternoon. I knew it was going to be tight in order for me to get to Billings in time for the concert.

To add to my frustration, on Friday afternoon when I checked on the status of the flight from Seattle to Bozeman, it was delayed. My stress level was growing. But then I began to think about how many times unforeseen circumstances like this had taken place before, and how God is bigger than any of these challenges or problems. So I prayed and asked the Lord to provide for my needs.

It wasn't far from my hotel to the Bozeman airport, and I made sure I was there before the plane was scheduled to arrive. I waited for my bags. Of course, they were among the last ones to come out. I grabbed them, headed for the parking lot, and began the 140-mile drive to Billings.

I left Bozeman at approximately 5:00 P.M., and the concert was to begin at 7:00 P.M. But with its open spaces and nearly empty freeways, the state of Montana allows you to travel over seventy miles per hour. I took full advantage of this—and then some. I stepped on it, to put it mildly. When I arrived in the parking lot of the church at Billings, I was told that there was a power outage in the area and we would not be able to start the concert until the electricity came back on. The extra few minutes until start time allowed me plenty of time to set everything up, get dressed, and prepare for the concert.

That night I drove back to Bozeman for a concert the next morning. Immediately following that concert, I drove 325 miles to my next concert in Kalispell. When I was pulled over for speeding, I feared the results: a heavy fine and points on my driving record back in Tennessee. I was delighted to learn that the fine was only twenty-five dollars and that Montana does not report speeding violations to Tennessee. I guess the lesson here is that if you are going to speed, do it in Montana!

By the time I returned to Bozeman on Sunday night, I had driven more than 1,100 miles in forty-eight hours.

In September 2008, I traveled to Bolivia with Dr. Frank González to provide music for a satellite evangelistic effort he had been invited to conduct in Cochabamba on behalf of La Voz. Frank was going to Bolivia directly from Southern California, where he lives. I was going to travel there from Chiapas, Mexico, where I would be for ten days of concerts as well as speaking to hundreds of young people at two retreats.

There was hardly any cell phone coverage where the retreats took place, much less Internet access. But somehow, I received a message, I believe on my cell phone, that my flights to Bolivia had been canceled. I immediately called Evelyn to find out what was going on and what I should do. That's when I learned that the country of Bolivia was close to civil war. Some of the governors were revolting against the federal government led by socialist Evo Morales, and all the major airports had been shut down.

It seemed that neither Frank nor I were going to be able to get to Bolivia for this important evangelistic campaign. Thousands of downlink locations around South America were waiting for these meetings to begin, but it seemed nearly impossible for us to be able to get there. All we could do was pray and put our trust in the Lord. But when we pray, hope, and trust in the Lord, we have at our disposal the most powerful Being in the universe!

One of my favorite stories in the Bible is found in 2 Kings 6:1–7. It is the story of the floating ax head. As a boy, I marveled when I heard this story and thought in wonderment how God could make something so dense and heavy float on water. And if God can make a piece of iron float, I am certain that He can solve my problems. The entire La Voz team was in prayer, as no doubt were dozens and perhaps hundreds of other people in South America.

Somehow, Dr. Frank was able to get into the country. He arrived at the location where the meetings were to take place and be broadcast a couple of hours before everything was to begin. I didn't get there in time for the first night, but I did arrive later that evening and was available to play for the rest of the meetings.

It was a truly crazy trip for me. I managed to visit four countries in less than twenty-four hours. With the help of some very creative agents at American Airlines, my trip was completely rearranged. I flew from Tuxtla Gutiérrez, Chiapas, to Mexico City on Mexicana Airlines. From there I flew to Miami on American Airlines and connected to Lima, Peru. I didn't sleep a wink on the flight even though my comfortable seat reclined fully into a bed. From Lima, I caught a puddle jumper belonging to some obscure little airline and flew to the border town of Juliaca, still in Peru. When I landed, somebody picked me up and drove me to the Bolivian border. After giving the border chief a generous tip, I was suddenly granted a visa to enter the country. Once in Bolivia, someone else was waiting to drive me to the capital city of La Paz, where I caught a flight to Cochabamba.

By the time I arrived in my hotel room around 9:00 P.M., I had been awake for close to thirty-nine hours. I was so exhausted that when I finally went to bed, my nervous system would jolt my body every few minutes and I couldn't fall asleep. Finally, I got up, filled the bathtub with hot water, and took a scalding hot bath, which relaxed my body enough to be able to fall asleep. I woke up the next morning just before noon. I had slept for more than twelve hours. I called Frank, we had lunch together; and in the afternoon, we headed for the auditorium where the meetings had already commenced. By the end of the week, more than six thousand precious souls had answered the call to accept the gift of salvation. All of the sacrifice and exhaustion had been well worth it for the glory of God.

In 2009, I visited Australia twice, in June and August. When I arrived in June, I learned that Melbourne was the worldwide epicenter of the bird flu virus. Not long before, when I visited Monterrey, Mexico, that had been the epicenter of the virus. Lucky me! After a concert at the Dallas Brooks Centre in downtown Melbourne, I met a beautiful couple, Johnson and Angie Alagappan, and they invited me to go to Albury, New South Wales, for a concert, which they quickly arranged to take place a few days later. Many area churches came together, and the concert was a great blessing. When I told them I was returning to Australia in August, they wanted to have another concert in Albury and a few more presentations in the area. So we made the arrangements.

My usual route when flying to Australia is from Chattanooga to Dallas/Fort Worth (DFW) to Los Angeles (LAX) on American Airlines, and then from Los Angeles to Melbourne, Sydney, or Brisbane on Qantas Airlines. The flight from DFW to LAX was delayed, which would make it difficult for me to catch my connecting flight to Melbourne and make it even more difficult for my bags to make the flight even if I did. So when I arrived at the American Airlines terminal at LAX, I raced to take the shuttle that would get me to the Tom Bradley International Terminal for the flight to Melbourne. I barely made the final boarding call.

When I arrived in Melbourne, I waited in vain for my bags at the baggage claim. I was going straight to Albury, which meant that Qantas would have to fly my bags there. There is only one flight a day from Los Angeles to Melbourne on Qantas, which also meant I wouldn't get my bags until the next day—right before the concert if I was lucky! I filled out all the necessary forms for my claim. Johnson and Angie picked me up, and we made the drive to Albury, with another friend who was coming with her daughter.

The seventeen-hour time change between the United States and Australia always staggers me; it takes me a few days to get used to it! So not long after we arrived at the home of Joe Pizzolato, a good friend of Johnson and Angie, I went straight to bed. I was absolutely beyond exhausted! The next morning, I wore a combination of borrowed clothes from Johnson and Joe in order to look presentable while playing special music for the morning service at church. By early afternoon, I was a bit frustrated that my bags hadn't arrived yet. The concert was set to begin, and I really wanted to wear my own suit. Still exhausted, I took another nap. When I woke up, lo and behold, my bags had been delivered! I only had an hour before the concert, but I was thankful God had allowed my bags to come in the nick of time!

One of the most thrilling and nerve-racking travel experiences that ever happened to me took place in January 2005. Evelyn had lined up two weekends of concerts in Oregon. For the second weekend, she booked concerts in Bend, Klamath Falls, and Forest Grove, near Portland. On the map, Klamath Falls doesn't seem that far from Portland, point to point. But the problem is that there is no straight shot between the two. I realized this the week of the concert, but by then it was too late to change the time, much less the date of any of the concerts.

Several Christian pilots lived in the area, and Linda Hill spent all week talking with most of them, trying to get someone to pick me up near Klamath Falls and take me to Forest Grove. But each had prior commitments or didn't want to risk flying that weekend, for a storm was predicted to come in. It seemed that all the doors were closing fast. The only thing left to do was to charter a jet. The pilots Linda had been talking to all flew turboprops. Jets can fly much more easily in inclement weather than can turboprops. We found a company that would fly me from Medford to Hillsboro. This would cost more than I'd make at the concert, but I had never canceled a concert before unless I was ill or because of bad weather, so I was determined to do what I had to do.

Linda called Brian Giles, pastor of the Forest Grove church, on Thursday to tell him about our dilemma. Sometime on Friday afternoon, he called her to tell her that his son, Matt, was a pilot and owned a small plane. Matt was a bit of a maverick and was willing to go pick me up near Klamath Falls and fly me to Hillsboro. I was relieved and excited! When I heard "small" plane, I prepared myself for a *really* small plane. But when I actually saw Matt's plane, I realized my expectations had been too high!

Matt flew down to a little airstrip at Modoc Point, about twenty miles north of Klamath Falls. After the worship service and concert concluded, one of the pastors of the church drove me to the airstrip. I arrived with most of my things, which didn't fit. So I had to prioritize—obviously, the violin, my briefcase, and me! That was about all that could fit. I don't even know what happened to my rental car and the rest of my things or how I caught up with everything later. But somehow, the Lord worked it out! I shook Matt's hand and thanked him profusely for his kindness. I continued to thank him the rest of the flight.

As we flew at a relatively low altitude, I experienced a calm and peace I hadn't felt in a long time. The only sound was the one made by the turboprop engine. Down below, was an evergreen winter wonderland. The ground and trees were covered with snow, and the fluffy clouds made it feel like I was in a dream. Occasionally, Matt would say something over his microphone, which I could barely hear inside my helmet. All my anxiety and stress about not getting to the concert simply faded away as I looked down at God's creation.

Matt's kit plane (yes, *kit* plane—he had bought the plane in pieces and assembled the parts) didn't have a big fuel tank; it didn't have anything that was big! So we landed in Bend in order to fill up the tank. When we took off, there were clouds everywhere. I don't know how fast we were going, but at some point, I thought we were going very slowly. There was a dense blanket of clouds, and I wondered if something was wrong. Suddenly, Matt pointed to his left. He was seated in front and I was behind him, so I had to rely on the microphone in my helmet to amplify what he was saying. All I saw was a window of clear sky opening between the clouds. Immediately, he made a left turn, and we headed for that clear window.

As we passed through the opening, Matt pushed the throttle, and we were going fast once again. He told me later that he had been waiting for an opening in the clouds. He didn't feel comfortable trying to break through the curtains of clouds, and if they didn't provide us an opening, we would have had to keep flying east and go north of Portland and probably around Mount Hood, then go west and turn south, in order to get around the clouds and make it to Hillsboro. It also meant I would've missed the concert!

When he explained this to me, I rejoiced and praised the Lord! We landed at the Hillsboro Airport around 4:30 P.M., and Matt's dad, Pastor Brian Giles, along with Herb and Linda Hill, were waiting for me. I gave Matt a big hug and thanked him once again. He took off and returned home to be with his wife and family.

We arrived at the Forest Grove church at 4:55 P.M. The concert was supposed to begin at 5:00 P.M., so you can imagine how busy we were, rushing around to get ready to begin the concert as soon as possible. The audience was patient as we dashed about; and within a few minutes, we were able to begin. The Lord blessed mightily that night. The impact and response from the congregation was powerful, and God's love and grace were manifested through His blessings! I have no doubt it was His way of reminding me that He is a God of possibilities!

Matt continued to pursue his passion for flying. It was evident to me when I met him that day, January 29, 2005, that he loved flying! Tragically, I later learned he died in a plane crash flying one of his aircraft. He left behind a beautiful family and a lot of broken hearts. I will always remember Matt for his kindness and generosity in taking time away from his busy life as well as his family to make it possible for me to share the love of God with the people of Forest Grove that night.

Standing with Matt and Pastor Brian Giles in Hillsboro, Oregon.

CHAPTER 11
ENFATICO
{Emphatically}

O ne of my favorite countries to visit is Australia. As much as I love the incredible landscape and the spectacular wildlife, I love the people even more! Aussies are friendly, laid back, hospitable, and have a no-worries approach to things. They don't get stressed out. I can't remember how many times I've told people in Australia about something that is concerning me, and hear them say, "No worries, mate." I love it! I love barramundi fish and chips! But when I go to Australia, it's not to be laid back! In 2007, I did forty concerts in forty-five days. I went to every state and territory in Australia except Western Australia. I was in Tasmania, but I never saw a Tasmanian devil.

In 2003, I met a couple, Graham and Barb Allen, who lived in Gosford, New South Wales. Graham was an Aussie, and Barb an American. They welcomed me into their home; and for the next several years, I'd stay with them when in the area. I grew to love Graham and Barb very much! In 2003 or 2004, after Graham had attended several concerts, he decided he wanted to sponsor an outback tour. He had seen the impact this music ministry had in reaching people for Christ and decided he wanted to bring these concerts to the smaller churches all around Australia—churches that were off the beaten path and that never got much of this kind of evangelism.

So in 2007, Graham took me everywhere: Cairns, Hervey Bay, Townsville in Queensland; Hunter Valley, Penrith in New South Wales; Alice Springs, Darwin in Northern Territory; Canberra in Australian Capital Territory; and Glenorchy,

Launceston in Tasmania among other places. I had the time of my life traveling with Graham. He had a passion for sharing Jesus with others. He had sponsored innumerable mission projects over the years and had built schools, churches, and many other buildings for God's kingdom. I saw alligator farms, the Great Barrier Reef, and the most spectacular starry nights in Tasmania. I rode a camel in Alice Springs, held koalas, and chased kangaroos. Many people accepted the gift of salvation at these concerts, and others renewed their commitment to the Lord. This is what it's all about!

In 2012, I received the heartbreaking news that Graham had been killed—struck by a vehicle while on a beautiful morning bike ride near his home. It was a devastating loss to countless people because Graham had touched so many lives!

On the outback tour of 2007 with Graham, we were about to jump on one of those small planes from one of those small discount airlines. When I presented my boarding pass, the agent told me I would not be allowed to take my violin on the plane. I assured her that the violin case would fit comfortably in the overhead bin. (In Australia, they call them "lockers.") But she said that it wouldn't, and she was not going to allow me to board unless I checked my violin.

Now let me tell you something, I can't and won't, now or *ever,* check my violin. That's just not possible. I don't own a Stradivarius, but I am very blessed to have an excellent instrument!

The prodigious violinist Itzhak Perlman has it written in his contract that he gets two first-class seats—one for him and one for his Stradivarius! Unfortunately, my contract doesn't include that stipulation.

It made me mad that the agent so incorrectly determined that my violin wouldn't fit when, of course, it would! Matters were escalating when Graham stepped in. With his calm voice and great sense of humor, he brought things back down to a normal conversation. Somehow, he was able to get the captain involved and infuse some reason into the situation. The captain, who is in charge of the aircraft and has the last word, opined that if the violin fit in the locker, it could be brought onboard. And after seeing how easily the violin slid into the locker, he let everyone know that all was well—"no worries." Graham saved the day!

In 2009, when my thirty-one-concerts-in-twenty-eight-days tour of Australia and New Zealand ended, I headed for the islands of Hawaii to do some concerts in Molokai and then take a couple of weeks to relax on the Big Island. I had corresponded with the Kaneshiros, a family from Molokai, who had invited me to come to Molokai to do a concert for the community. This family loves the Lord, is very musical, and are beekeepers. Denny, the father, had sent me some shipments of their honey, and it is truly fabulous! I love the slogan that appears on all their products: "To God Bee the Glory." That is just fantastic! Denny began to study and play the violin as an adult, which isn't easy. Yet he's done well for himself.

When I left New Zealand and arrived in Honolulu, I experienced the most drastic time change ever—twenty-one hours! I left Auckland on Monday, September

21, around noon, and arrived in Honolulu on Monday, September 21, around 9:00 A.M., a difference of twenty-one hours. But in reality it was only a three-hour time change (like going from my home in Tennessee to California). The twenty-one-hour change in time between New Zealand and Hawaii is due to the fact that they lie on opposite sides of the international date line. At any rate, I was exhausted not only from the long flight but from a very busy tour.

This had been my third trip to New Zealand and my second time staying in the home of Alistair and Paula Smith. Staying with them was like being right at home. They are lovely folks who treated me better than I deserved! Their children, Kyle and Tamzin, play the violin and cello, and I enjoyed having them perform at some of the concerts. My last concert that weekend was in Whangarei, on the north tip of North Island. On the way up, we passed a lot of (you guessed it) sheep farms. Paula let me get out of the car and chase some of the baby lambs until I finally caught one and took a picture with of me holding it. The lamb was so beautiful! Once while I went chasing after lambs, the owner of the farm came out and chased *me* off the property! That was a hoot!

I arrived in Molokai, Hawaii, early in the afternoon, and Denny was there to pick me up. He and his family had arranged for me to stay right on the beach in the guesthouse of some friends. Let me tell you, it was just what the vacation doctor ordered! The concert at the Lanikeha Community Center wasn't until the twenty-third, so I had two days to relax and recharge. It was no more than a fifty-foot walk to the beach since the property was right on the beach. I could wake up from a nap or take a break from practicing, and within a few steps and a matter of seconds feel the white, powdery sand and crisp, clean ocean water.

There's something about the sand, the sun, and especially the ocean that invigorates me. I was a sickly boy, but my mum is convinced that spending summers at the beach in Varadero in the central province of Matanzas in Cuba is what cured me. As exhausted as I was when I arrived at the Molokai guesthouse, I felt energized as soon as I went out to the water. The ocean also helped me to relax, wind down, and sleep like a baby that night. The windows facing the ocean were open, and I slept to the sound of the waves gently rolling on to the sand, and the wind caressing the palm trees and branches.

I think the Kaneshiros could tell how exhausted I was. They picked me up for breakfast, lunch, and dinner, and then brought me back to the guesthouse shortly after each meal. Instead of going for a run along the snakelike road, I decided to jog along the beach. I even went into the water about knee deep and jogged that way. I was getting a great workout when all of a sudden my left foot came down on a sharp piece of coral just below the ball of my foot and the arch. I saw all kinds of stars at that moment, and I yelled loudly. But there was nobody to hear me. In fact, I never saw a soul along that strip of beach and vacation homes during the three days I was there—except for Wednesday. And that story is coming up! I didn't think my gash was going to require stitches, but it was going to prevent me from running every day as I had planned. When I go on vacation in Hawaii, one of the nonnegotiable activities is running every day. During my twenty-eight days of concerts in Australia and New Zealand, I been able to go running only once—in Port Macquarie. That day, I managed to convince my hosts, James and Julie Chissell, to drop me off at the beach and pick me up a few kilometers up the road. So when I arrived in Hawaii I was in need of some good exercise. Now, my cut foot might cause me to lose three or four days of the two weeks I was going to be in Hawaii on vacation after Molokai.

The Kaneshiros have a beautiful family, and the children are sweet and gentle. So when I arrived for dinner and announced that my foot had a small hole, the children began to mobilize. I don't know what they treated my foot with— something with a combination of antibacterial, balm, and rejuvenating properties. But I can tell you that by the time I left Molokai for Honolulu and Kona, I could run again. But the thing that remains indelibly printed in my brain was the prayer that one of the children prayed. Before they applied all the remedies, one of the daughters prayed and asked Jesus to heal me. She said that without His intervention what they were about to do to help my foot might not be effective. It blew me away that even in connection with something so basic as a home remedy, those children prayed over the wound in my foot and asked Jesus to heal me. I learned later that if the cut wasn't properly cleaned, the coral could grow inside the wound after it closed up.

One of the most bizarre, hilarious, and embarrassing things that ever happened to me took place on Molokai on September 23, 2009, hours before a concert. As I mentioned earlier, I hadn't seen a soul along that area during the three days and nights I was there. And since I pretty much had my own private beach, I decided to go skinny-dipping and tanning, if there's such a thing as "skinny-tanning"! I had always heard of skinny-dipping but had never dared to try it. But this was the perfect place. There were trees right off the beach and no one around for miles. So I went out, had a good look around to make sure nobody was there, went into the water. After checking for peeping sharks or dolphins, I took off my swimming trunks when I came out of the water and lay on the sand sunbathing.

Of course, I kept my swimming trunks right beside me just in case a large bird happened to fly anywhere close. Every few seconds, I opened my eyes apprehensively, to make sure I was the only creature around. But after a while, I relaxed. I was lying sideways on the sand so that the waves that came onto the beach would splash the entire side of my body, and I would be refreshed.

And then things went wrong! After a few minutes of calm and peace, I had a weird feeling, so I opened my eyes. When I looked over toward the ocean, I saw a kayak way, way off in the distance. It had to be a half mile away, and I didn't think anything about it. Actually, what I thought was this: *It can't possibly be that out of the entire strip [no pun intended] of beach along this area, the kayak and whoever is inside it is going to come anywhere close to me!* And so I closed my eyes again.

A few minutes later, when I opened my eyes again, I could see two kayaks, and I could hear male and female voices. I could hardly believe it, but it almost seemed that the kayaks were pointed directly at me. A bit alarmed but trying to assuage my fears, I told myself, *There's no way in this world that those people are headed my direction!* But just in case, I grabbed my trunks, which were two feet to my right, and covered myself with them. *These folks probably haven't even seen me lying here,* I told myself. A few minutes later, I opened my eyes again and was flabbergasted to see that the two kayaks were making a beeline for me.

What am I going to do? I asked myself. I couldn't jump up and run toward the house at that point. I'd moon them! I had left my towel on the picnic table about twenty-five feet away. So I decided to put my arms down at my sides, so that if they did come any closer they'd see my trunks on top of me and my arms around my sides, and wouldn't think anything was wrong.

At this point, I didn't even want to open my eyes! The laughter from the two couples in the kayaks had disappeared as they approached me, and I could just feel the tension in the air. I barely opened my left eye, trying to have a peek, hoping they were paddling past me on their way to Maui or somewhere. To my amazement, the two couples disembarked about ten feet from where I was lying. When I opened my eyes to talk to them and try to excuse myself, I could tell they were as uncomfortable as I was! Apparently, they had parked their car in the driveway of the property where I was staying, as they knew the owners of the place, and had gone out into the water and were now coming back.

I remember mumbling something like, "I'm so sorry! I've never done this before, and I didn't think there was anyone around." Needless to say, they were not amused. They picked up their kayaks and walked around me as far away from me as possible, loaded up their car, and drove off. My face looked like a tomato. My first skinny-dipping experience would be my last!

In 2007, I went to eastern Europe on a concert tour with the Baptist Missionary Association of America. I had met Brother Jerry Kidd and his wife, Sue, at a retreat in Branson, Missouri, in May 2003. We hit it off instantly and over the course of time grew to be very close. Within his organization, Brother Jerry was in charge of large territories around the world, including eastern Europe. He and Sue had been missionaries in Bolivia for many years, and they have a passion for souls. Given his vast experience reaching people for Christ, he approached me about doing something different—using music as a way to reach people. In many parts of Europe, people just aren't very interested in spiritual things. But they love good music. Brother Jerry envisioned doing a concert tour to several countries in eastern Europe and then sharing with people about Jesus during the songs (just like I do in the United States and around the world).

The results were marvelous! People filled the venues and not only heard good music but also our testimony and God's Word. At these concerts, people would accept the gift of salvation and experience changed lives. Others reaffirmed their faith and commitment to the Lord. Young people dedicated their talents for God's glory. From 2007 to 2010, I did a ten-day missionary concert tour in eastern Europe every summer. Brother Jerry was with me in 2007 and 2008.

The first year we had concerts in Romania, Austria, Czech Republic, and Ukraine. The next three years we focused on Ukraine. On Wednesday, June 13, 2007, I flew from Chattanooga to Chicago and then to London Heathrow, and finally to Budapest, Hungary. I arrived Thursday afternoon in Budapest pretty tired. I'm one of those unfortunate souls who hardly ever sleeps on a plane. So I was eager to collect my luggage, head to the hotel, take a shower, brush my teeth, put on some fresh clothes, and relax before going to sleep. But when I went to claim my luggage, it had not arrived. I had flown to London on American Airlines and then changed to Malév Hungarian Airlines. It's not uncommon when you fly on different airlines on the same trip to have your bags miss connections somewhere.

Brother Jerry, who was accompanied by Brother Larry Barker and Brother Danny Bagosi, told me that there would be another flight coming from London that night and that hopefully my bags would arrive before we started for Oradea, Romania, the next morning. Brother Jerry was in the same boat as me—his luggage hadn't arrived either. So we went to grab something to eat, and then we headed to our hotel to rest.

The next morning, we returned to the airport to check on the bags. There was good news and bad news. The good news was that the bags had, indeed, arrived the night before. The bad news was that somewhere along the way, probably in London, someone had ripped open my duffel bag, removed all the contents, and sent the empty bag on to Budapest. Quite a bit of that kind of thing goes on in big airports. Tens of thousands of bags come through every day, and baggage handlers who scan the bags through the X-ray machines can see if there are valuable electronics in the bags. Laptops, iPads, iPhones, and many other articles disappear from bags. Recently, I read of a baggage handler at the Minneapolis–St. Paul International Airport who was arrested for stealing more than seven hundred items, valued at more than eighty thousand dollars, from electronics to guns, over the course of eight months. I also know someone who flew to Europe and made the critical mistake of placing cash inside a book in his checked luggage. When he arrived at his destination, the money was gone. I don't know what the person who stole the contents of my bag saw, because other than an electric shaver, I didn't have any other electronics. Despite the inconvenience, I didn't lose things that were irreplaceable.

When we arrived in Romania, I went shopping for some of the things that had been stolen: dress shoes, toiletry bag, clothes, and so on. We had a very busy and blessed weekend with seven presentations from Friday night to Sunday night. Some of these were church concerts, another was a church dedication, and one was a special program for missionaries and local pastors. The Lord blessed our efforts, and His name was glorified!

From Romania, we drove back to Hungary. During a day off, I was delighted to be able to meet with László Samu and his wife, Gabby, while in Budapest. László had been the orchestra manager of the Hungarian National Philharmonic Orchestra in 1999 when I flew to Budapest to record my *Christmas in the Aire* CD. I had not seen or communicated with him since then. We shared a lovely afternoon tea by the water before I headed to Vienna.

One of my favorite cities in Europe is Vienna. It seems that every building there is beautiful and ornate, and the cultural and musical history is awe-inspiring. I remember walking along the winding cobblestone side streets in 1992 when an older gentleman came up to me and took me to a quaint café. In his limited English, he said, "In this coffee, Mozart and Beethoven." I was there along with Stephen and Paul Tucker as well as Dan Pabón to record an album. I don't know if we looked like musicians or if he had an arrangement with the café whereby he received some sort of remuneration for bringing in business. And I will never know if Mozart and Beethoven truly visited that café, but the thought of it was tantalizing enough that we wanted to go inside the café!

Brother Jerry is a godly man and a true servant of the Lord. I've never seen him get upset, lose his patience, or respond to someone by treating them in an unloving fashion. The only time I ever heard him raise his voice in righteous anger was when two Gypsy teenagers tried to pick his pocket. They nearly had his wallet in their hands! They had circled us a couple of times and had figured out that his wallet was in the right outside pocket of his very light jacket. Then they moved in to execute their plan. One managed to distract us by showing us a map and pointing to it, and the other gently slid her hand inside the pocket of Brother Jerry's jacket. Thankfully, he realized what was going on just as her hand was pulling the wallet out of his pocket. And he rose up and rebuked them. But even then, I noticed he did so with kindness.

Of course, while in Vienna, I had to go to Starbucks and get a mug. I collect these from all the countries I've been to—those that have Starbucks. Brother Jerry, Danny, and I walked all around Vienna during the couple of days we were there.

After our concert in Vienna, we headed for the Czech Republic to do a concert not too far from Prague. There was a volunteer student missionary (VSM) group from the States in the small town of Jílové, reaching out to the young people there, and our concert helped to bring in more people. After that concert, we headed to Prague to do some sightseeing before going to Ukraine for the last leg of our missionary tour. Prague is a spectacular city, replete with musical and religious history and culture. It was in Prague that Reformer Jan Hus (John Huss) began to preach at the Bethlehem Chapel against the practice of his church selling indulgences. That was pretty bold, considering he was the dean of the Charles University in Prague. He was excommunicated by the pope in 1410 and was burned at the stake as a heretic in 1415.

One of the landmarks of this spectacular city is the Prague Clock Tower, which has been around for more than six hundred years. Every hour on the hour, doors open, and figures of the apostles rotate for a short period of time.

But in spite of its many cathedrals and churches, including the large monument to Hus in the middle of the Old Town Square, Prague is one of the most secular cities I've ever seen. Brother Jerry, Danny, and I walked around at night sightseeing, and I was absolutely astonished to see tens of thousands of young people seemingly endlessly wandering about the city. Brother Jerry told me that he'd seen this many times before, and it made him weep. In one of the most beautiful cities of this world, most of the young people wander around without purpose or plan, looking for perhaps pleasure and enjoyment that fade away before the night is over. I wondered how these young people could be reached for Christ!

On June 22, Brother Jerry and I flew to Kiev, Ukraine, for the last leg of our tour. Our plane was scheduled to arrive at 11:30 P.M., but due to flight delays, we didn't get in until 2:30 A.M. Poor Brother Jeff Franks, who was picking us up, had to wait endlessly. When we finally arrived at the Kiev Boryspil International Airport, it was a free for all to get in line for immigration. I had never seen anything like it. People flocked to the lines in front of the cubicles where the immigration officers sat. Three or four people at a time would be pushing and shoving, trying to be next in line to see the officer. I was so tired, I wasn't in the mood to push or shove, so I was probably one of the last to go through.

When I went to the baggage claim area, my luggage had not arrived. So there was another delay as I had to wait in line at the claim office to file a report. It was probably 3:30 A.M. or later when we finally left the airport. It was a short night, and I was exhausted when I woke up. We had a concert that evening, and so we had a number of things to do, including buying some decent clothes for the concert, since all I was wearing was jeans and a T-shirt. As tired as I was, Brother Jerry and Brother Jeff had to be even more tired, for they had gone to bed later than me and had risen earlier. But they never complained. They were happy and anxious to minister to people at the concerts. They were a great example for me, as I tend to be a bit grumpy and curt after a short night.

When we went to the center of Kiev, I was shocked to see so many luxury cars—Maybachs, Bentleys, Ferraris, Rolls-Royces, 7 Series BMWs, 600SEL Mercedes, and so on. In the span of perhaps twenty minutes, I saw at least one of each of these cars driving around. I asked Brother Jeff if Ukraine was car heaven or if everyone was rich. He explained to me that these cars belonged to the wealthy, ruling class (a.k.a. Mafia) and that they had plenty of money at their disposal. After the fall of communism in 1989, a new kind of communism sprang up: the rich and powerful became richer and more powerful, and the poor became poorer.

We visited the square where tens of thousands had gathered during the Orange Revolution of 2004–2005, peacefully protesting and showing their dissatisfaction with a corrupt government. When Viktor Yushchenko was declared the winner of the presidential election on December 26, 2004, there was excitement and hope that the new president would govern fairly and justly. But unfortunately, as time went by, things returned to being the way they had been before.

When we arrived at the church in Kañiv, an able and expert sister helped alter my newly purchased pants and shirt, shortening the length of my pants and shirtsleeves, so I didn't play the concert looking like a walking laundry basket!

At that very first presentation in Ukraine I immediately noticed how much Ukrainians love music. They listened intently and seemed to take in every note, every phrase, every word my violin was saying. It wasn't difficult for me to understand parts of the Ukrainian culture, given my background coming from a communist country. In addition to the winters being brutally cold, people became cold and hard on the inside because communism attempts to strip everyone of privacy and individuality in an effort to indoctrinate everyone that the state is more important than the individual. But as the people spend time with you and trust you, they open their homes and their hearts and make you feel right at home.

In fact, Brother Jeff coined a term that became an inside joke for us: "terrorist hospitality." When we arrived somewhere before or after a concert, it didn't matter how tired we were or how full we were from having eaten already or what our plans were, we were going to be received and entertained by the pastor, a family, or church group! Even after Brother Jeff told the pastor that we had a long drive ahead of us following the concert, we were invited to mingle and eat with the brethren. And we couldn't say No—to say No was to offend them. And no matter how exhausted we were, we really didn't want to offend our brothers and sisters who had prepared a small feast for us.

One time, Brother Jeff and I were invited to stay at the home of a lovely family. We had driven several hours to get to the church and arrived barely in time to set up the sound and begin the concert on time. Afterward, we just wanted to go to sleep as soon as possible. But when we arrived at the home of this hospitable family, it became clear that we would not be able to excuse ourselves and retire for the night. The man of the house brought us into the living room, gave us cookies and tea, and began to engage us in conversation. At one point, Jeff and I began to nod off. We were simply exhausted. When the man of the house realized this, instead of sending us to bed, he got up, turned on all the lights in the living room, and announced, "This is so that you don't fall asleep during our conversation!" Brother Jeff and I remember this story and talk about it almost every time we're together.

During the tours of 2007–2010, I spent countless hours with Brother Jeff driving all over Ukraine, sharing music and testimony with thousands of people. I loved every moment as I grew to know, appreciate, and respect this man of God. We had concerts in Odessa, Vinnitsa, Lviv, Lutsk, Yalta, Sevastopol, Alushta, Simferopol, Donetsk, Mariupol, Dnepropetrovsk, and, of course, Kiev, to name just a few places.

But back to our tour in 2007. Our last concert took place on June 25; the next day I was to fly home. Jeff would have liked me to stay an extra day to go around Kiev, do some sightseeing, and visit his home in Bucha. But I had a concert in Oregon on June 28 and had to come home to unload and reload before heading to the next destination. Very, very early on June 26, my flight left for Paris on Ukraine International Airlines. I had a long seven-hour layover in Paris before boarding an American Airlines 767 to Chicago, and then finally on to Chattanooga.

When I arrived in Paris, I made my way to the Admirals Club lounge and was able to take a little nap for a couple of hours. Even though I was tired—I had to get up that morning at 3:30 A.M. after going to bed around 11:30 P.M. the previous night—the nonreclining seat in the lounge didn't allow me to rest comfortably. So I got up and walked around the inside of the terminal, visiting the duty-free shops, killing time, shopping, eating, and waiting for my flight to board. Those seven hours seemed like a week!

Finally, I made my way to the gate area to get ready to begin boarding. Everything seemed to going smoothly; passengers were boarding without delay, and bags were being loaded smoothly and efficiently. I had been sitting in my comfy seat with my seat belt strapped around me for only about six minutes when the captain came on with an announcement. "Ladies and gentlemen, *mesdames et messieurs*," he said, "we have a problem." Now I have been flying long enough to know that when the captain says, "We have a problem," he isn't talking about a lightbulb that just went out. When you're flying, you do *not* want to hear the captain say, "We have a problem!" So I knew we were in for it.

The captain went on to explain that one of the maintenance employees had managed to punch a hole in the belly of the plane in the process of trying to attach a hose in its proper place. Crews had already tried to solve the problem, but the hole was too big, so they couldn't fly the plane. Fortunately, he said, there was a spare 767 nearby, and the airline was in the process of making the switch from one plane to the other. All of us would have to get off the plane, and the bags would have to be unloaded, so they could tow the disabled plane to the hangar. Then they would bring in the other plane, reload the bags, and reboard the passengers. As you can imagine, this process wasn't going to happen in twenty or thirty minutes. It ended up taking almost two and a half hours—the exact amount of time I had to make my connection between planes in Chicago!

When I finished doing the math, I realized that unless my flight to Chattanooga was delayed, I was going to miss it. And that flight home was the last flight of the night! The next flight to Chattanooga wasn't until the next day in the early afternoon. However, I needed to be on a US Airways flight the next day in the morning, going to Boise, Idaho. If I missed my flight home Monday night, I'd miss my Tuesday morning flight, and I wouldn't make my first concert in Oregon. But instead of worrying as I often do, I prayed right then and there, and asked God to provide a way for me to get home that night.

I prayed, "Lord, You can delay the plane in Chicago." It seems that when you want or need a flight to be on time, it's delayed. And when you want it to be just a little late, it's on time! I can't say I heard God's voice in answer to my prayer. But at that moment, I had a sense of peace and calm overtake me that I believe was the Lord impressing me that everything was going to be all right. I thought about the situation once or twice during the flight from Paris, and I prayed. But for the most part, I let the situation go and trusted in the Lord.

When I arrived in Chicago's beautiful international terminal (Chicago is my favorite city in the world) and deplaned, the first thing I did was to look at the monitors for flight information. I wanted to see what was happening with the flight to Chattanooga. To my utter delight, I read that the flight was delayed forty-four minutes! Now, forty-four minutes isn't a long time at all when you're going from an international to a domestic connection. But I simply took the delay as an encouraging omen that God would work out the rest. So I did my best to get through immigration and customs as quickly as possible!

Those were the days before Global Entry kiosks and the Trusted Traveler program allowed you to get through the process of immigration and customs much faster. But I still managed to pass through quickly. It was one of those days at O'Hare International Airport when the lines were long everywhere. Even the line outside customs to recheck your bag was ridiculously backed up. So I took the bag with me and onto the train to terminal 3—the American Airlines terminal. When I arrived there, I went to a ticket counter, explained my situation to an agent, and was able to turn in my bag there.

American Eagle flights depart mainly from the G concourse in terminal 3, so I went to that security checkpoint, which is usually less crowded than the others. When I got through security and corralled my violin and briefcase, I began *running* to my gate because it happened to be gate G19A—the gate furthest from security in the G concourse! When I finally got there, I was relieved to see "my" American Eagle Embraer jet parked outside the jet bridge. However, the agent wasn't at the door of the jet bridge; he was working on the computer under the G19A sign. Out of breath and rushing, I reached his station and whipped out my boarding pass. "I'm probably your last passenger," I said.

"No, you're not," he replied. "I've already closed out the flight. It's too late."

I tried to get him to change his mind. "Please, sir, let me get on the plane. I've got to get home tonight. And I'll be seated with my seat belt on in no time at all." I was hoping he'd soften up and let me get on the plane.

But he was immutable! "Sorry. It's too late."

I was frustrated, but I didn't give up. I ran back to the Admirals Club, close to gate G7. Week in and week out, you'll find me there during layovers. Chances are, I know the agents working there, regardless of the hour. When I arrived at the Admirals Club, I began to tell an agent my situation and story. In between deep breaths, I talked as fast as I could. He took pity on me and rang gate G19A. The agent who had denied me boarding answered immediately.

"I have a passenger in front of me who just came off the delayed flight from Paris, and he really needs to be on this plane headed home tonight." I was listening intently and watching the face of the agent for any expression that might tell me what the other agent was going to say. Instead, I *heard* his reply: "Sure, send him down this way."

Whoa! The agent in the Admirals Club must have had the Midas touch. But I wasn't about to complain. As he handed me back my boarding pass, I picked up my violin and briefcase, put them around my shoulders, and made a beeline to the gate.

As I was approaching the gate, I saw the agent—the one who had denied me boarding just a few minutes earlier—opening the door to the jet bridge. I thought to myself, *Thank You, Lord!* But when he opened the door, he walked in, turned around and looked back at me, and closed the door behind him, leaving me *outside* the door! I touched my arms and face to make sure I hadn't drunk Kool-Aid recently that had made me invisible. I stood there speechless. After about four minutes, the agent returned, calmly opened the door, *saw* me standing in front of him, didn't say a word, *closed* the door behind him, left me standing there, and walked back to his computer. Exasperated, I raced back to the Admirals Club to talk to the nice, helpful agent I had spoken with just a few minutes before!

When I arrived, he was surprised to see me. "What happened?" he asked.

"I don't know. Perhaps I was invisible or I looked at him the wrong way, but he didn't let me board."

Now the agent was a bit ticked. He picked up the phone and rang the same gate agent once again. "Why didn't you let my passenger board?" he asked.

Once again, I *heard* the other agent's response: "Tell the passenger that if he gets here in the next thirty seconds, I'll let him board. The plane is about to push back."

As I dashed out, I said to the nice agent, "Thank you! Thank you! Thank you!" This time when I arrived at the gate, the agent had the door to the jet bridge open and was standing behind the boarding pass scanner. I handed him my boarding pass, he scanned it, gave it back to me, and I ran down the jet bridge as he closed the door behind me.

When I reached the end of the jet bridge and turned left (it was so long it seemed I was running to Chattanooga), there was my American Eagle plane! It was six feet in front of me. It was beautiful! *But,* there was an agent standing between me and the door, and the door to the plane was closed. I don't know if you're aware of the fact that during the boarding process, agents can open and close the door to the jet bridge, or gate, multiple times. But once they shut the door of the plane, there is no reopening it except for an unusual circumstance or occurrence. I know this very well, so when I saw the door to the plane closed, my heart absolutely sank! All this running around for nothing? So close, and yet so far? I was discouraged.

The agent in front of me was on the phone, and as she looked me up and down, she said to the person on the other end, "I'm sorry, but nobody told me another passenger was coming. I've closed the plane door, and the plane is leaving."

When I heard those words, I nearly lost it. I had been awake for twenty-three hours and had been rushing around back and forth the last few minutes. I took my frustrations out on the Lord. I closed my eyes and said irritatedly, "Lord, I thought You *told* me I'd get home tonight. But look, the door is closed. It's too late!"

Foolish me. Of course, God knew what was going on. Of course, He could see that the door to the plane was closed.

But what is a closed door to God? Nothing more than an opportunity! A couple of seconds after I said that prayer, I realized my lack of faith. I closed my eyes again. "Lord, forgive me for not trusting You. I know You can stop this plane from leaving. But if it's not Your will that I get on this flight or if You choose not to intervene, I know that Your plan is perfect! Amen." I stood there for just a few moments, collecting myself. I had run as fast as I could to get to the gate, and I was almost hyperventilating. Perspiration was dripping from my forehead.

The agent went back and forth with the person on the other end of the phone, and then she hung up. At that point, I expected her to tell me to return to the gate and speak to the gate agent. But to my amazement and pleasant surprise, she looked at me and said, "Sir, you must know somebody, because they told me to open the door of this plane just for you!"

Hallelujah! The Lord had worked it out! She opened the door, and I walked on to the plane, stowed my violin, slid the briefcase under the seat in front of me, sat down, and fastened my seat belt. All within thirty seconds or less. I had made the flight!

When I arrived in Chattanooga and went to collect my luggage, it had not arrived! But that was fine with me. I was home, and I had options. The next morning when the Hamilton Place Mall, which is close to home, opened, I was there at Mori Luggage to purchase a new garment bag. I came home, packed, and headed to the airport. I made my flights on US Airways to Charlotte, Phoenix, and Boise. And I made it to my first concert in Oregon!

When the agent in Chicago told me, "You must know somebody," I knew she figured that because I'm a very frequent flier with American Airlines I must have made a phone call to a friend, a supervisor, or a lead agent to get help. And in turn, that someone helped me to get on that plane. But what she didn't know was that the person I know is God Himself. He can remove any mountain or obstacle. He can do what nobody else can do! If He can part the Red Sea, He can solve your problem! I am learning, day by day, to trust Him first and foremost and to go to Him first. If you have a problem, don't go to a friend or a relative or someone of power and influence. Go to the most powerful Being in the universe, God Himself!

Putting on a Chapel program at Gilson College, Victoria, Australia, 2009.

Sydney Harbor Bridge, 2009.

Wahroonga, Sydney, 2009.

Holding a lamb in New Zealand.

One of many sunflower fields in Ukraine.

In Kiev with Brother Jeff Franks.

With Brother Jerry Kidd (Hawaiian shirt) and Danny Bagosi (behind me in the light shirt) and Volunteer Student Missionary team in the Czech Republic.

With Brother Jerry and Sue Kidd, December 2011, Arkansas.

With friends Herb Hill and Michael Roberts in Queenstown, New Zealand.

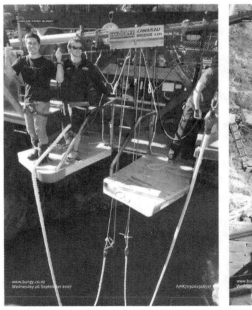

Kawarau bungee jump, Queenstown, New Zealand, 2007.

CHAPTER 12
SFORZANDO
{Made Loud; A Sudden Strong Accent}

It makes my blood boil when Americans and Canadians come up to me and say, "I went to Cuba last year, and I had such a great time. The country is beautiful, and the people are so happy."

My response, as gently as I can manage it, which isn't always so gentle, is as follows: "They take you to the tourist spots so you see only the things that aren't falling apart. And when you are in a hotel, restaurant, or store, a five-dollar tip equals a half-month's wages. So don't you think that every Cuban who sees a tourist is going to smile, hoping you'll tip him?" Come on!

Every trip I've taken to Cuba has been a tremendous encouragement and blessing as well as heart wrenching. To see the faith and trust that many of my Cuban brothers and sisters have in the Lord, despite living in a country where most people make ten or twelve dollars a month and have nothing, is awe-inspiring. Seeing how little they have and how they try to survive will make anyone ashamed of the fact that we are so blessed (and spoiled) here and how often we complain about so much!

There's been an embargo against Cuba by the United States since the early sixties. After President John F. Kennedy betrayed the Bay of Pigs invasion and Castro's stranglehold on the island was solidified, the United States established an embargo in order to isolate Castro and pull the financial oxygen out of the regime, hoping it would lead to his downfall. Unfortunately, fifty years later, it still hasn't worked. The only people who have been affected by the embargo are the citizens of Cuba. Castro has everything he wants. So I don't support this useless embargo that has not fulfilled its intended results.

You can't just go to Cuba from the United States if you decide you want to. But if an individual or organization obtains a license from the U.S. Treasury Department to travel there for humanitarian, missionary, or even artistic or cultural purposes, they can travel to Cuba. This is how I have been able to go a number of times in an effort to continue supporting God's work in Cuba.

Recently, music superstars Jay-Z and Beyoncé traveled to Cuba for their wedding anniversary. A whole lot of hoopla was made about it. I don't support those kinds of trips because first, it gives other people the impression that things in Cuba are OK; second, it legitimizes the oppressive regime in a way; and third, the people of Cuba don't benefit from it. When filmmaker Michael Moore went to Cuba and marched into a hospital, video crew and cameras in tow, to capture and praise the virtues of free health care in Cuba, he was ignoring the truth and the facts that most Cubans have little to no health care at all. Sure, health care is free in Cuba. But there's nothing to receive or obtain. Some of the most basic medications, such as antibiotics and even aspirin, are next to impossible to find in Cuba.

When former president Jimmy Carter went to Cuba and paraded himself walking down the streets of Havana with Fidel Castro, it only legitimized Castro's oppressive and murderous regime. The hospital that Michael Moore visited was a hospital for tourists and military personnel. Now, if you're one of those individuals, then your health care is excellent, and I might even dare say, among the best in the world. But if you're a Cuban, you get nothing. One time I asked someone in Cuba, "When you get a headache, what do you do?" His answer? "Wait for it to go away." When I go to Cuba, I go with my bags full of such things as toothbrushes, aspirin, T-shirts, sandals, shoes, and so on. When I come back, I come back with empty bags because I give everything away. People ask and beg for the most basic things.

Why certain people turn a blind eye to reality or even distort the truth, I don't know. Cuba is not a desirable place to live. In fact, unknown numbers of people risk their lives every day to leave Cuba and come to America—getting on inner tubes, man-made rafts, canoes, and so on, and trying to paddle, row, and even swim the shark-infested Gulf of Mexico. That is how desperate they are to leave the country. Have you ever heard of Americans trying to cross the border into Mexico or get on a raft to go to Cuba because things here are so bad? I don't think so! That tells you the whole story.

Let me tell you about a friend of mine, Luis Gomez. My family and I lived across from his family's house in Santa Clara, Cuba, when I was a boy. After my family left in 1980, I didn't see him for more than twenty years. When I returned to Cuba in 2001 for the first time, I saw Luis in Havana. He told me of his burning desire to bring his family to the United States. I tried everything I could to bring his family here through the proper channels, to no avail. It seems that many Cuban people who want to come to America legally can't. There's a law—an unfair law, in my opinion—that any Cuban who touches American soil is automatically granted asylum. I say that it's an unfair law because I don't know of any other person coming from any other country who has that same opportunity. This law probably stems from the colossal mistake of the United States in betraying the Bay of Pigs invasion and a bit of guilt on the part of those responsible for this betrayal. So millions of Cubans dream of being able to touch the sand of the Florida's beaches because they know that once they do they have a brand-new lease on life. It reminds me of the sick woman who wanted only to touch the cloth in Jesus' coat, certain she'd be healed!

After trying and trying for years to leave Cuba, Luis finally figured out a way. He sold his beautiful 1957 Chevy and somehow got a visa to go to Uruguay with a friend. They were promised (by whomever they paid to help them) that once there, they would receive a visa to go to Guatemala. But the visa was not issued. They lost their money and were stuck. But like most Cubans—who can reinvent the wheel, make sandals out of two by fours and dice using melted plastic from molds improvised from aluminum soda cans, who make skirts out of the cloth from potato sacks, and who manage to survive every day when it seems impossible to survive—Luis and his friend, after surviving on the streets for thirty days, found a way to get a visa to Guatemala on their passports and airline tickets to that country.

When they arrived in Malacatán, Guatemala, and attempted to cross the river into Tapachula, Mexico, they were kidnapped by the Mara Salvatrucha gang. Their captors stripped them down to their underwear, bound them, and threw them in a hut. Their chief, Catalino, told them to call their friends or relatives and tell them to send five thousand dollars each for the two of them by Western Union or the gang was going to kill Luis and his friend. Luis told Chief Catalino that they had no families in the United States, that they had left their families behind in Cuba in hopes of reaching the United States and one day bringing their families to America. So Chief Catalino told them they'd rot and die in that hut.

For five days, they were held captive in the hut, hoping, praying, and waiting upon the Lord to deliver them. Every day, Chief Catalino would come and ask them if they were ready to call someone in the United States and have the ransom sent. All they were fed those five days were corn tortillas and water. Finally, on the fifth day, Chief Catalino told them he was going to leave them there to die. My friend Luis said to him, "You can leave us here to die, but my heavenly Father will deal with you for your sins."

When a couple of other gang members heard Luis talking about God and sins, they went over to talk to Chief Catalino. Luis could make out part of the conversation that went something like this: "The cops are all over these mountains looking for us, and if we harm these Christians, we might be cursed by God. Just let them go and die on their own in these mountains." So Chief Catalino came, cut the ropes that bound Luis and his friend, gave them back their clothes, and sent them away.

When they arrived in Tapachula, Chiapas, which is just about the southernmost point in Mexico, they were without money to buy the bus tickets that would take them all the way to the border town of Matamoros, Nuevo León, which is just about the northernmost point in Mexico, across the Rio Grande from McAllen, Texas. My friend, Luis, prayed, and someone bought them the bus tickets they needed, along with the necessary visas to get through Mexico on that bus. This person also told them to make ten to fifteen photocopies of this visa because as the bus traveled through Chiapas, the police would periodically stop the bus and ask every passenger to produce paperwork. They would demand a bribe or tear up the visa. Then if Luis and his friend had no visa the next time the bus was stopped by the police, they'd be pulled off the bus and sent back to Guatemala.

The Mexican government turns a blind eye to its citizens crossing the border illegally into the United States. But if you are in Mexico illegally, the authorities will immediately arrest you and deport you. The police at Mexico's southern border with Guatemala are famously brutal, beating and torturing illegal aliens trying to cross into Mexico from Central and South America, and even raping the women.

I want to loudly note and proclaim here that the things I've just mentioned should not be considered a reflection upon the wonderful citizens of Mexico. I have traveled to Mexico more than fifty times in the last nineteen years, and in few places around the world have I met people who are as kind, generous, and giving as the people of Mexico. In few countries have I been as well received as in Mexico! Mexico is one of the most beautiful countries in the world and astoundingly rich in natural resources. But it has a very corrupt political system, and its politicians pilfer the natural resources, take advantage of millions of hard-working Mexicans, and amass huge fortunes and great power for themselves! It breaks my heart to see these things! I love Mexico and its people, and Mexican food is my favorite food!

So my friend Luis made several photocopies of the visa. At every random stop, he and his friend were asked for a bribe or, as they say in Mexico, a *mordida,* which means "bite." In other words, the police want a "bite" out of your apple, your pie, your income. At every random stop, they told the cops they didn't have any money, and at every random stop, their visas were torn up. Fortunately, they made it out of Chiapas with a couple of photocopies still in their wallet, and from that point on, they weren't asked for the visa.

All the way to Matamoros, Nuevo León, they rode on that bus. And when the bus finally stopped, they went straight to the border. They hadn't eaten in a couple of days as they didn't have any money. When they presented themselves at the United States border and declared themselves to be Cubans and showed their passports, they were immediately arrested as a matter of procedure. They were taken to an office, and not long after, a U.S. Border Patrol officer came in with sacks of McDonald's value meals. He announced that they were now in the

United States of America and that they would be well treated and fed.

And so one sunny afternoon in 2006, when I was in California having lunch with Bob and Cindy Carmen, a couple I stay with just about every time I'm in the Sacramento area, I received a call from my friend Luis telling me that he was in the United States of America. Immediately, arrangements were made for him to travel from Texas to southern Florida, where he began a new life, with new energy, hopes, and dreams of working hard, making an honest, decent living, and bringing his wife and children here. Though the last few years haven't been easy, he's managed to accomplish all of the above.

If that doesn't say it all about this country (the way they were treated and fed at the border), I don't know what does! Even when you're illegal, you are treated with respect. This generous, selfless spirit is what has made this country great. But so many try to take advantage of it, and I hear so many people say that because this country was founded by immigrants, anyone that wants to come here should be able to come with no problem. That's crazy! I am an immigrant. I am a beneficiary of this country opening its arms to me. But my family came here *legally*. I give back to the system. I pay taxes. I give back to my community and country. I am not a drain on this country. Recently, a friend of mine said to me, "Last year, I paid one hundred thousand dollars in taxes, but I didn't see the benefits from the taxes I paid." And then there are people who don't put anything into the system, yet they take advantage of the system, use and abuse it, while not putting in their fair share. Want to talk about fair share? Why do those who work hard and make money have to pay for those who don't? I believe in giving. I give tithes and offerings; I give to charities; I give my time, energies, and resources to help others. But I shouldn't be forced to pay something unreasonable to make up for the fact that others aren't contributing.

Dr. Ben Carson, who I am privileged to know and call a friend, said recently at the 2013 National Prayer Breakfast that if 10 percent is good enough for God, it should be good enough for the government. Dr. Carson is someone who came from nothing. He lived in the projects of Detroit. He wasn't expected to do anything with his life. But his mother ingrained in him the importance of an education and reading. So he read, and he got an education. And today, Dr. Ben Carson is not only one of the top pediatric neurosurgeons in the world, he has a foundation that helps countless young people get ahead in life.

We are becoming a nation of spectators. Instead of getting involved by giving, volunteering, helping, and educating, we are satisfied when we are told others or the government will do it. We have become a nation of couch potatoes. We believe what the mass media tells us without finding out for ourselves. It sounds good when we hear some politicians say they are looking after the needy, the disadvantaged, and so forth. But it almost sounds like these socioeconomic problems are the fault of those hard-working people who get ahead in life and that they should be penalized and "pay their fair share." Instead of creating a mentality of entitlement, we need to create a culture of improvement, growth, education, empowerment, and accountability. Margaret Thatcher once said that the problem with socialism is that you "always run out of other people's money."

In his stirring song "Imagine," John Lennon wrote about a world where there was no greed, no hunger, no possessions, just a brotherhood of all people. Of course, all of us would love to see every person, especially every child, in this world have enough to eat. We'd all like to eradicate hunger and disease! In regard to possessions, the funny thing is that Lennon was one of the biggest capitalists of them all! He would never share his nearly billion-dollar fortune with other people. Some say he didn't even leave anything in his will to his first son, Julian.

America is broke—sixteen-plus trillion dollars in debt. Not because we don't tax the rich enough, but because we spend more than we bring in. Europe taxes everyone to the limit. In some European countries, you'll pay a tax rate in excess of 60 percent. And yet Europe is still broke! If you take the incentive away from people to work hard, they will stop working. And then who will pay for those generous benefits that the unemployed receive? When François Hollande ran for president in France, he ran on a platform that included instituting a 75 percent tax rate on anyone making over one million euros a year. Interestingly enough, the tax revenues from this measure would have raised a few hundred million dollars, which wouldn't have even put a dent in the 110-plus billion euro deficit for just one year.

Two summers ago, a friend of my mother's visited her in Charlotte, North Carolina. My mother, along with her friend and my sister, came to visit me in the Chattanooga area for the Fourth of July. My mom's friend left Cuba more than thirty years ago and went to England. I was shocked to learn that since arriving in England, she's *never* worked a day in her life. The government gives her certain welfare benefits, and she has learned to live within those means and has not needed to work, because she lives off the government. We were having a conversation one afternoon, and I'll never forget what she said. "In England, there are many opportunities, because there are many benefits. But here in the United States, you have to work."

Imagine that! Imagine having to work for a living! I was floored. A good friend of mine, Randy Finnell, had invited us to spend the Fourth with him on his boat on the lake at the Chattanooga Yacht Club (CYC). This was the second or third time Randy or Ray and Ann Barr have invited me to the CYC. And they always ask me to put on a concert for the people that gather there. I do that happily, and I end with a patriotic medley and ask everyone to sing. After the concert, there's a great big lunch that everyone enjoys.

My mom's friend had a fantastic time eating, riding on the boat, seeing the fireworks, and sharing an amazing day. She was also amazed to see such beautiful boats, houses, and cars. I guess if you choose not to work, it's amazing to you to see what happens when you work hard, live on a budget, save money, and share with others. Every year, I hear how the national deficit is going up, and I hear politicians talking about cutting the deficit and balancing the budget, while others continue to ignore it—and they all wind up increasing the deficit in the end. Something has got to give!

I met a girl in Toronto, Canada, several years ago at a concert, and we've become good friends over the years. She has a love for Jesus and a passion to help others. She volunteered her time as a missionary and has done many things to help others. And like most people educated in Canada's schools, she had this romantic vision of socialism. She wanted to go to Cuba on vacation. So I gave her some tips on where to stay, what kind of transportation options she would have (renting a car, hiring a taxi), what churches she could visit, and so forth. When she returned, she sent me this text message: "I had the time of my life in Cuba! Totally fell in love with the sun, sea, and people. . . . And yes, though they have less, the way of life. . . . Granted, I don't know the details or the religious context, but I do think their simplicity and the lack of materialism is truly liberating in a way I don't even think they understand." She acknowledged that she didn't know the details, but she felt certain the people of Cuba feel liberated because they don't have much.

This was my response: "*Hmmm.* We see that perspective from here. But their simplicity and lack of materialism is forced upon them. Their consuming concern is to eat and survive. After that, they are forever and desperately [attempting] to acquire the things that we have here and take for granted. With all their simplicity and lack of materialism, they are even more unhappy than we are. There are those who are resigned to hopelessness, and the spark of life in their eyes is gone. When I go to Cuba, people ask me nonstop for money, food, clothes, medicine. There is a balance to strike between abundance and scarcity. Money can't buy happiness, but it is a vehicle. I work so hard, in great part, so that I can help others who are in such need."

Let me give you some details as I did for this girl. When I was in Santiago de Cuba several years ago, a gentleman came up to me after the concert. He said to me (and I memorized and burned his words in my mind): "I'm ninety-three years old, and my brother is ninety-five. We live in a hut with a dirt floor. We have nothing to eat, no money, and no medical care. But I still have dignity. Can you help me?" Even as I write these words and remember this encounter, I have tears in my eyes for two reasons: (1) the thought that these two brothers lived in such abject poverty and yet managed to hold their heads high, and (2) the fact that I was on the tail end of my trip and had given away every last dollar I had. I had nothing to give him and no way of ever finding him again. Imprinted in my mind is the picture of this short gentleman who was missing most of his teeth.

Now let me give you some religious context. This is the story of Roberto Martín Pérez, a friend of my father's, who spent twenty-seven years and ten months in jail in Cuba. Roberto's dad was a high-ranking official in Castro's regime, but Roberto turned against the regime and planned a failed *coup d'état*. In jail, he met a young man by the name of Olegario Charlotte Espileta, who was thrown in jail because he was a Christian. The jail was shaped like a cylinder, with a spiral stairway in the center. Every so often, the guards would organize a *paliza,* a beating or pummeling of the prisoners. A certain whistle would sound, and the prisoners had to strip, run down the stairs, and go through this line. On both sides of the line, were guards with bayonets, clubs, bats, knives, and other weapons. The prisoners had to run through the center of that line as the guards took swings, swipes, thrusts— whatever they could and wanted to do.

Roberto says that sometimes prisoners died before coming out of the line, eyes were ripped out of sockets and lay on the pavement, heads and skulls were shattered, and so forth. And while that was happening downstairs, other guards were going through all the prisoners' few belongings in their cells and often destroying most of them. For a long time, Olegario had managed to keep hidden a New Testament in his block. Every day, when the political prisoners returned from forced labor, Olegario would take out his New Testament and say, "My lion cubs, come gather around me and let me read to you the Word of God." But on this day, Olegario didn't have enough time to hide the New Testament before having to run downstairs and go through the *paliza.* And the guards found it and confiscated it.

When the prisoners returned to their cells and gathered their things, Olegario noticed his precious New Testament was gone. And so he asked to speak to one of the guards. When the guard came, Olegario told him that the New Testament must have been taken by the guards and that he was beginning a hunger strike immediately until they returned it to him. The guard relayed Olegario's words to the reeducation officer, and he came and told Olegario that he would be placed in solitary confinement so he could have time to think about his hunger strike.

Olegario was six feet, six inches tall, and the solitary confinement block was about four feet wide and five feet high. The first three inches above the block were covered in excrement, urine, blood, and so on, from the other prisoners who had been there before. The block hadn't been cleaned in a long time. So Olegario had to kneel, squat, and sit there. He lasted forty-seven days in that filthy dungeon on his hunger strike, and then he died. Roberto says that after a couple of days, the prisoners noticed the smell of Olegario's decomposed, decaying body. And they began to rise up. Roberto became the ringleader of this uprising. The prisoners screamed, yelled, and threw things at the guards. One of the supervisors came in and fired his machine gun at random, spraying bullets everywhere.

A bullet ripped off one of Roberto's testicles. As he was bleeding, the guards dragged him by the arms and threw him in the same solitary confinement block where Olegario had died. They had removed Olegario's body, but they hadn't cleaned the block. They left Roberto in that cesspool of germs with an open wound. He thought he was going to die. But then he determined that he had to live through this in order to tell the world what was going on in Castro's jails.

The one thing that all prisoners had and carried with them everywhere was their spoon. This is how they fed themselves when they ate. So Roberto began to run the aluminum spoon against the wall of the block quickly and repeatedly until it became extremely hot. Then he'd press the spoon against the open wound in his scrotum in order to cauterize the wound and keep it from getting infected. This is how he survived.

Like Roberto Martín Pérez and Olegario Charlotte Espileta, there are thousands upon thousands of people who have harrowing stories about their lives under Castro and communist Cuba. And imagine the thousands who died or were killed whose stories aren't known. There are millions of people whose lives have been destroyed by that murderous regime. Families have been torn apart forever. In Cuba, there are roughly eleven million people who are currently looking forward either to coming to the United States or just dying.

So when people talk to me about the virtues of the Cuban government or the way of life there, where everyone is equal and how wonderful communism and/or socialism is or how happy Cubans are, I hope you can understand why I can never stay silent on the issue. And I hope you can understand better why I cannot agree with former president Jimmy Carter walking the streets of Havana alongside Fidel Castro, or Jay-Z and Beyoncé going there on vacation, much less Michael Moore falsifying the truth, or even those who are genuinely misinformed.

On paper, socialism is the greatest thing in the world! Everyone shares; nobody is without; and the wealth is spread around. The only problem is that it *never* works that way. In countries such as Cuba, Venezuela, the former Soviet Union, and so on, you have extreme socialism and communism, where the dictators have everything, and everyone else has nothing. Then there's western Europe, where in France the unemployed have unions that fight for more unemployment benefits, and other countries have "free" health care and other social benefits. But workers make very little and have very little. The houses (mostly apartments in buildings in the cities) are very small and old; everything is expensive; and many services outside of public transportation, which you pay for, are deficient.

When I go to Cuba, my business is not with the government. It is simply to help bring hope and salvation through Jesus Christ to the people of Cuba, so that they may have the assurance that, at least one day, they will be free when they get to heaven!

Luis with his '52 Chevy.

The '52 Chevy.

With friends Robert and Cindy Carmen in Northern California.

Receiving a gift from the governor of Vera Cruz, Mexico, Fidel Herrera.

CHAPTER 13

DOLCISSIMO
{Very Sweetly}

Since my first trip to Cuba in 2001, I've had a passion for supporting God's work there! So it's been a privilege to work with different churches and denominations in coordinating various mission projects for that country: printing Bible lessons, sponsoring pastors, bringing in "the Jesus Film," delivering funds to build and remodel churches, obtain basic equipment, buy Bibles, and so on. And my friend Luis, while he was still there, was always a huge help. Luis is the kind of guy who knows everyone on the street. If you needed to find something, he could help you. As we'd drive down the street, people would shout out a greeting from the sidewalk, inside a house, or outside a store. Luis was a huge help!

One time, my good friends, Dr. Steve Peterson and Trent DeLong accompanied me to Cuba. They were able to get through immigration and customs OK, but I got stuck inside. Because I was born in Cuba, I have to travel with a Cuban passport when I go to that country. It's the only place in the world I know of (other than Bolivia and Venezuela), where I can use my Cuban passport. Otherwise, it's worthless! And on top of that, I need a special, religious visa that the government issues. But that visa must be brought to the airport, and when I present myself at immigration after the flight arrives, I have to wait for the immigration officer to go to Arrivals, yell out my name, and the person with my visa hands it to the agent. Then he or she will return to where I am and process me into customs. Sound cumbersome and inefficient? It is!

So this time I went to a cubicle, presented my Cuban passport, and told the officer that someone should be outside with my visa. The officer went out and yelled my name for my visa. Nobody came forward. So he came back and said I'd have to wait. It was very late in the evening, as the flight had been delayed. In fact, I was the only person waiting in the immigration area. Nearly a couple of hours passed. Luis, who was waiting outside for me, began to call around to see who might have my visa. He finally spoke with a pastor by the name of Alejandro Morgado, who had it. But he had arrived from another part of the island and was in bed and didn't want to go to the airport. He figured I could wait until the next morning. So did the immigration officer. At one point, I saw all the lights starting to be turned off. I learned later that everyone was going to leave me there and close the place until morning!

My friend Luis jumped in his car and drove to Pastor Alejandro Morgado's house to get the visa. Fortunately, Pastor Morgado didn't live too far from the airport. When Luis returned, he asked to speak to an immigration officer. He was told that the immigration office was closing down. He explained that I was still in there and that he had just brought my visa. The officer told him that he was going home and that he would be back to process my entry in the morning. That's when Luis did something crazy. He said to the officer, "Do you have any idea who you have locked up in there?"

The officer said, "No."

Luis told him, "The person in there is a violinist coming here to do special programs at the invitation of Raul Castro. If I tell Raul that you left him there to sleep on the floor tonight, he'll have you thrown in jail before you report to work tomorrow morning."

I was cracking up laughing as Luis told me the story later! Apparently, it worked. All of a sudden, the place lit up like a Christmas tree. Agents started taking their places at the baggage claim and customs. The immigration officer walked in, motioned for me to go with him, and within ten minutes, I was out of immigration and customs with all my bags! In Cuba, after leaving immigration, it's usually an ordeal to get through customs. There have been times when the customs agents have opened everything I brought and have gone through every single article of clothing, crevice in my bag, and anything else they can think of. It normally takes two to three hours.

When I finally walked out of the airport, Steve, Trent, and Luis were anxiously awaiting my appearance! When I translated the story to Steve and Trent, they could not stop laughing.

It was on this trip that I met Lissette. As Steve, Trent, Luis, and I went around to the different home-churches, meeting the laypastors and church pastors, we were taken to the home of a very special laypastor—Lissette. She was born with cerebral palsy; her speech is barely understandable. In fact, it's understandable only because her mother translates for her. Her eyes are terribly crossed, and her movements are nearly out of control. If she wants to sit, she asks her mother to sit her up. If she wants to change positions, her mom has to do it. Basically, she can do next to nothing by herself. But even that condition has not stopped her from reaching people for Christ!

She recited for us all sixty-six books of the Bible by memory and in their correct order. She read to us out of her Bibles. She had different ones, and they all look like accordions, because when she tries to turn the pages as she's reading and studying, she rips and crumples them. As impressive as all this is, that's not all!

Lissette's mother took us outside their house, which is on a street corner. A lot of people walk in that area. Right next to the front door of the house are two chairs. Every day, Lissette asks her mother to pick her up and carry her to one of those chairs. And as people walk by, inches from her, she extends her arms and folded hands and calls out to them, inviting them to sit next to her and study the Bible. When someone heeds her call and accepts her invitation to sit next to her, she begins to talk to them about Jesus, with her mom translating! At the time I met her, she had brought twenty-seven people to Jesus Christ! Hallelujah!

Doesn't that inspire you? Perhaps you have tears running down your cheeks like I do right now. Lissette's story is inspiring, motivating, challenging, and it probably puts most of us to shame! Because if she can do that, then certainly I can do so as well! And if I can do something to bring people to Jesus, then certainly you can too!

There's one more story I want to share with you about Cuba. Back in 2008, a missionary, evangelistic effort was planned that involved, I believe, more than 220 different set of meetings all across the island. There were four big meetings in Guantánamo, Santiago de Cuba, Santa Clara, and Havana. I accompanied Pastor Frank González for part of those meetings. Twice a night, he would preach in two different churches. The churches were absolutely jam-packed. The aisles were completely filled with people sitting on the floor; the hallways outside were standing room only; and there were people hanging from the windows outside looking in.

This story takes place in Santiago de Cuba. We had requested that the government give us permission to use a public venue that seated three thousand people. If the government said Yes, it would be nothing short of a miracle! We waited and waited and waited for an answer. On Monday, four days before the meetings were to begin, we finally got word that we would be allowed to use the auditorium. On Wednesday evening, the speaker arrived in Havana. Thursday morning, he was required to meet with the highest ranking official in Cuba in charge of religious affairs. From the moment the meeting began, the tone was negative.

"Why does the United States have an embargo against Cuba? Why do you support that embargo? Why do you and your country want the people of Cuba to suffer?" The religious affairs officer rattled off these questions in rapid-fire form, not really looking for answers. When she finished asking questions, she announced, "I'm in charge here, not God. Forget about using the auditorium for the meetings beginning tomorrow."

Now it was the speaker's turn to answer. "I don't want the people of Cuba to suffer. And I don't preach or talk about politics. I only talk and preach about Jesus, because He's the only hope we have. I want to thank you for your time." And he got up and left.

What were we going to do? It was just over twenty-four hours until the meetings were to begin. Three thousand people were walking, riding bikes and horses, driving cars, and traveling in buses—all to attend these meetings. And now we didn't have a place to hold them. The speaker began to gather pastors to pray. God really was, and is, in charge! He could exercise His power and intervene. So they continued praying.

An hour after they had been praying without ceasing, the phone rang. It was the head of religious affairs in Cuba, and she wanted to talk with the speaker. "Sir, I listened to what you said, and I've been thinking about it. I have decided to change my mind. You can use the auditorium as previously granted for these meetings. And because I know that you people like to baptize, I've authorized the use of an Olympic-size swimming pool very close to this auditorium, so that at the end of your meetings, you can have a place for the baptism. Goodbye."

Wow! Can you stand up with me and glorify our heavenly Father? Can you say with me "A Mighty Fortress Is Our God"?

At the end of the meetings, more than a thousand people were baptized in that swimming pool, including a man in a wheelchair who had to be lowered into the pool with ropes. In total, more than 5,100 people (as I shared in chapter 9) were baptized all across Cuba during these coordinated meetings. Praise the Lord!

As much as I wish I could give everyone enough money to help them substantially, it is impossible. And while I do what I can, what brings me even greater joy is to be able to help bring the kind of hope and joy that is truly everlasting! I know the Lord has called me to continue to support God's work in Cuba as long as I breathe!

Six members of our family arrived in the United States in 1980: Pipo (Dad), Mima (Mom), Maydelé (my sister), Leonel (my uncle, and Mima's brother), Bayba (my maternal grandmother, Eneyda Díaz), and me. I don't know how May and I nicknamed our grandmother, but we must have done so early on. Interestingly, we never really wrote out her name, we just said it in conversation. A few years ago, I wrote out "Bayba" when referring to her. But May spelled it "Vaiva" when she wrote it out. Since then, May and I have had an ongoing discussion as to which spelling is correct. Since this is my book, I get to spell her name *Bayba*!

I have a fairly small biological family: my dad was an only child, and my mother had just one sibling, Leonel. By the time I was born, my paternal grandmother and maternal grandfather had passed away. I look forward to meeting them in heaven. I was fortunate to know my maternal great-grandmother, who we called "Abuelita Nina." Though small, our family has always been unified.

In October 2003, I was in Southern California recording a new CD, *Softly and*

Tenderly, volume 1 of Simply Classic Hymns, when Pipo called to tell me that his dad, my grandpa, had passed away at the age of ninety-three. "Abuelo," as May and I called him, always found a way to get us things few people in Cuba seemed to find—certain foods, toys, clothing, and so on. He had a big house that May and I loved to visit, right behind the baseball stadium in the city of Santa Clara. When my family came to the United States, he decided to stay in Cuba. Twice, in 1983 and 1987, he and his wife, Rafaela, whom May and I called "Nena," came to visit us, both times in Chicago. I got to see him twice when I began to travel to Cuba starting in 2001.

I was returning home in March 2007, when Mima called to tell me that Bayba had passed away at Leonel's home in Miami Beach, Florida. She was eighty-nine. Our family immediately traveled to Florida so we could gather together and have a memorial service. Bayba was the perfect grandmother—sweet, loving, wise, and hilarious. She was truly the center of attention when our family got together, and we loved hearing her stories and jokes and laughed with her.

I miss Abuelo and Bayba immensely, and I look forward to seeing them in heaven!

Almost every year, our family gathers at my house in Tennessee for Thanksgiving and Christmas. With all the traveling that is part of my life, the last thing I want to do is to have to get on a plane to go somewhere for those special holidays. So my family indulges me by coming to my place. In addition to that, I try to see the family a few times throughout the year. May and I have gone on vacation to Hawaii several times as well as to such places as Spain, on a cruise to Alaska, and so on. In 2011, I took Mima and May to the Napa Valley for a wonderful week of vacation. We visited all around the area as well as San Francisco and a number of other places in Northern California. May, Leonel, and I have planned some special trips with Mima in the next couple of years. Pipo has enjoyed going on a number of mission trips since his retirement, and because he's retired, I get to talk to him just about every day.

In 2010, I fulfilled a twenty-one-year-old dream! Many years ago, an article appeared in one of the *American Way* magazines (the publication of American Airlines) about the biggest tomato fight in the world—La Tomatina. It takes place in the town of Buñol, just outside of Valencia, Spain, on the last Wednesday of August every year. May went with me, and we had an absolute blast being covered in tomato pulp from head to toe, along with about forty thousand other people!

Because of my constant travel and concert schedule, I always look forward to the special family gatherings and activities planned, especially around the holidays. My biological family on this earth may be small, but my family in the Lord is huge!

Jaime, May, Mima, and Leonel, Thanksgiving 2009.

With May after the tomatoes had flown.

CHAPTER 14

LEGATO
{Joined; Smoothly; In a Connected Manner}

The most powerful force in the universe is love. The Bible says in 1 John 4:8 that God is love. And I believe that music is the second most powerful force in the universe. Without saying a word, a tune, a song, or a melody can bring me, and probably anyone else, to tears. Music can make my heart beat faster or slower; it can make me want to dance or simply relax; it can change my mood and do many other things. Music allows me to communicate, share my heart and thoughts. In a way, music allows me to speak. It is the international language, and everyone can understand it!

I believe God created music for two primary reasons: (1) so we could praise, worship, and glorify Him; and (2) so we could communicate and fellowship with one another, even when we might speak different languages. It wouldn't take much to figure out what a huge part music plays in my life.

Music brings us together, but it can also divide us. Entire churches, even families, have been split because of music. Some folks like the old hymns; others like the new songs. I've shared music in churches during the last year that have combined both styles in worship. I think of the huge Church of the Redeemer in Gaithersburg, Maryland, where my friend, Brian Taylor, is the worship leader. This church has five services every weekend, and it utilizes a mix of contemporary music and old hymns. The Arlington Seventh-day Adventist Church in Texas has services using different styles of worship and music. When I was there recently, I played one style of music for the traditional service and another style for the contemporary service. Just a few weeks ago, I was at University Baptist Church in Houston, Texas. I've been there twice now, thanks to my friend Jim Smith, whom I met several years ago when he was the minister of music at another church in the area. For the traditional service, I played in the orchestra. Matt Marsh, the associate pastor and worship director, who's a true artist, led the choir in a sublime fashion. I had goose bumps on my skin as well as tears in my eyes at times. For that service, I was dressed up in a suit with a shirt and tie. A couple of hours later, the choir was gone, along with the orchestra. A rug was brought in; cables, in-ear monitors, and amps adorned the stage. And the contemporary worship director, Ben Sandstrom, led the music. I changed into less dressy clothes, and away we went.

Despite the gallop toward contemporary worship services and music over the last ten to fifteen years, I think I'm seeing a bit of a return to those old hymns that direct our thoughts, praise, and worship to Jesus Christ. My aim here is not to set up a list of guidelines as to what is, or is not, good worship music, or what is, or is not, good music. I simply want to remind us all of the importance of music in worship and in our lives.

I think of the ABBA song "Thank You for the Music." The lyrics include the following lines:

> Thank you for the music, the songs I'm singing;
> thanks for all the joy they're bringing.

I believe that Benny Andersson and Björn Ulvaeus, the composers of this song, were acknowledging that their gifts and talents were given to them by God. Over and over again, when we read the Psalms, many of which were songs, we see the caption "To the Chief Musician."

We've read many times the story about David playing his harp and the evil spirit in Saul leaving him (see 1 Samuel 16:16, 23). We've heard about the "new song" in Revelation 14:2, 3: "And I heard a voice from heaven, like the voice of many waters, and like the voice of loud thunder. And I heard the sound of harpists playing their harps. They sang as it were a new song before the throne, before the four living creatures, and the elders; and no one could learn that song except the hundred and forty-four thousand." We probably remember the Song of Moses in Exodus 15, and that the redeemed will sing the Song of Moses and the Lamb (see Revelation 15:3). In fact, the Bible is replete with references to music in worship.

As I visit churches, one of the clear indications to me that a church is thriving is that it makes music an integral part of the service. There are so many churches that use music as filler and so many pastors who diminish the role of music in the worship service, perhaps because they're afraid of the power of music. But I want to encourage you to use music as a way to worship the Lord.

I want to give you two very different examples from the Bible regarding the use of music. You're probably very familiar with the first one, but perhaps you haven't thought of it in musical terms. When mighty King Nebuchadnezzar wanted to make people bow before the huge golden image he had constructed and worship it, he asked the orchestra to play a song. I often wondered why he did that. Was it because he didn't want people to be distracted by all the noise the tens of thousands, perhaps hundreds of thousands, of people were making as they were kneeling? Was it just because he wanted something to fill the gap between his speaking and their kneeling? I don't think so. I believe this use of music was a very calculated move on his part. There were probably many people in that crowd who didn't want to bow down and worship that image. Having so many people bow down was going to create a logistical mess for Nebuchadnezzar and his soldiers to arrest those who remained standing and take them to the fiery furnace to destroy them.

I believe the reason King Nebuchadnezzar had an orchestra play at this crucial time was to convince—perhaps hypnotize—the masses into kneeling! I imagine that the composer of that music created such a mystical, ethereal, intoxicating sound through the components of melody, harmony, and rhythm that any resistance to the king's command the people may have had was completely overcome and they were brought under the total control of the king's irreverence.

The second biblical example of the use of music that I want to share with you is one I've never heard any preacher, or even musician, talk about. It is a story found in 2 Chronicles 20. What's happening here (see verses 1–13) is that three nations have united to destroy Judah, and there is great consternation and distress on the part of God's children. Then the Holy Spirit comes upon Jahaziel (see verses 14–20), and he encourages the people and tells them to trust in the Lord, assuring them that He will fight on their behalf. And this is where the story gets exciting!

When the people of Judah get ready for battle, they do something drastically different than you might expect! Instead of sending the army (air force and marines), they send out the choir (see verses 21, 22). Yes, the choir is sent out *in front* of the army to sing and to praise. How would you feel if the president of the United States (or the leader of your country) called your church and asked you to be a part of a choir that was going to stand in front of the army in a battle and sing? You might not consider this to be the ideal spot for an audition for *American Idol*, right? But that's what happened in this Bible story. Let's read these verses:

> And when he [Jehoshaphat] had consulted with the people, he appointed those who should sing to the LORD, and who should praise the beauty of holiness, as they went out before the army and were saying: "Praise the LORD, for His mercy endures forever."
>
> Now when they began to sing and to praise, the LORD set ambushes against the people of Ammon, Moab, and Mount Seir, who had come against Judah; and they were defeated (verses 21, 22).

Did you catch that? Not a single arrow was shot, not a single bullet fired, not a single grenade lobbed. When the people sang and praised the Lord, the opposing army was utterly and totally defeated! The next few verses outline the incredible spoil that Judah carried home as a result of completely routing the enemy (see verses 23–30). What does that tell me? It tells me that while I am singing and praising the Lord, no matter whether in the car, the street, the store, the shower, or the gym, my act of worship in music is so powerful that it can prevent the devil from harming me even before he attempts to do so. It stops Satan in his tracks. That sounds like a pretty powerful tool to me!

I always try to have a song of praise to God in my heart and my mouth. And I encourage you to use music to praise the Lord constantly. The more you sing, the more God will surround you with His love, Spirit, and protection! The more songs of adoration and praise your church sings, the greater the presence of the Holy Spirit in that worship.

I just received an e-mail from someone I made friends with many years ago in Brazil. She attended one of my concerts in the southern state of Rio Grande do Sul. We stayed in touch and then lost touch for fifteen years. Recently, we reconnected. We caught each other up on our lives, and then she went to our Web site and YouTube to listen to our music. She wrote, "I'm crying as I watch your videos. I must confess that it's been years since anything has stirred my emotions and connected me to God as much as your music is doing. . . . Because of the twists and turns of life, I've not been to church in many years. . . . Watching and listening to this music, has filled my heart with joy for God."

Many years ago, when my family lived in Chicago, my father told me the story of someone to whom he had given a copy of our CD *We Shall Behold Him.* My dad, Pipo, didn't know the internal struggle that person was experiencing. He didn't know that this person was planning on taking his own life that night. This person decided to play the CD as he prepared to take his life. But the Holy Spirit used good music to reach that desperate soul. As he began to listen to the music, he was filled with peace and calm. When the CD ended, he played it again, and he began to pray. He continued to play the songs on that album until the urge to take his life was gone and new feelings of hope, trust, and joy in the Lord filled his heart. His life became a witness for the Lord!

Music has that power to bring people to Christ. Music is physical as well as spiritual. And when used for His honor and glory, it can touch the heart and stir the soul like, perhaps, nothing else. Of course, the wrong kind of music can have devastatingly negative effects. But I want to concentrate on good music, music that praises the Lord. I believe that when we get to heaven, we will all play instruments. In Revelation (see Revelation 5:8; 14:2; 15:2; etc.), an instrument that is often mentioned is the harp. I don't know if these references are to literal or symbolic harps. Of course, I would like to ask the Lord to give me a violin! And I am certain there will be a heavenly orchestra and choir. I plan on being a part of that orchestra. Whether you have a musical talent here on earth or not makes no difference. In heaven, you will sing and praise the Lord as if you had been studying music your entire life!

I urge you to make a habit of using psalms, hymns, and spiritual songs, as Ephesians 5:19 puts it, in your everyday life, in order to praise and worship the Lord. When you sing to the Almighty, you are summoning the most powerful Being in the universe to your side! And as you sing, you will experience the love, calm, and confidence in God that will allow you to say, "It is well with my soul," no matter what happens in this life!

CHAPTER 15
CON FUOCO
{With Fire}

I was on a cruise with my sister, May, in 2011 when she suggested doing something to celebrate twenty-five years of our music ministry. I had been invited by Calvin Knipschild, my friend and music director of Christian Edition, a men's chorus, to be a part of that group's thirtieth anniversary celebration. We almost didn't make the cruise! I had concerts in Albuquerque, New Mexico, on June 17 and 18 and was going to catch the first flight to Dallas/Fort Worth and on to Vancouver, British Columbia, where the cruise was to begin. May was coming from Charlotte, North Carolina. We were both going to cut it close as it was, because we were to arrive about two hours before the cruise ship was to depart. Any flight delay or backup at immigration, and our cruise would be in peril.

I woke up early on the nineteenth and headed to the Albuquerque airport. I turned in my rental car, checked in for my flight, went through security, and waited to board. Everything went smoothly. I arrived in Dallas/Fort Worth on time and boarded my next flight. But instead of pushing back from the gate, we just sat there. We were delayed about thirty-five minutes. May's flight was delayed, too, as I found out later. So now I had about an hour and a half from the time the flight arrived in Vancouver until the cruise ship left the dock. And I still had to go through immigration, customs, and get to the dock!

On one occasion several years earlier, it had taken me more than two hours to get through immigration at Vancouver International Airport. When the lines are full, it seems like you are a quarter of a mile from the immigration kiosks. This time, when I came down the stairs and into the immigration hall, the lines were all the way to the end. I knew I wouldn't make it to the ship on time if I waited in line. So I prayed for charisma. I began to talk to people who were in line asking them to let me go through. Somehow, I made my way to the front of the line. As I was getting ready to walk up to the immigration agent, I noticed a gentleman whom I recognized. This retired physician and his wife, from the Denver area, had sponsored me many years before while I was in medical school. They were in Vancouver with their granddaughter to attend our cruise! Now there would be four or five people who might "miss the boat," so to speak.

I sent a text to May telling her to just go, if she wanted to, but she waited for us. When we finally got our bags (another slight delay), cleared customs, and met outside, we had less than forty-five minutes. Even without traffic, it could take as much as thirty minutes to get to the dock. We piled all our suitcases and bags in the trunk of the limo, and the five of us climbed in, prayed, and the driver took off. I can tell you that I was pretty worried, and I talked nonstop (imagine that)!

When we arrived at the place to check in for the cruise, they were starting to close the lines. Thankfully, we got through. May and I were the last passengers to walk up the gangway and onto the ship!

We had a fabulous time being a part of this cruise, seeing friends, and making new ones. Every day, we would have a program for our guests, and the rest of the time, we did whatever we wanted. We had a blast! My close friend Bob Norman and his wife, Jan, were among the guests that had come along, and we all went on bike rides, shopping, and even rode a zip line during the stops in Canada and Alaska.

May suggested we should have a cruise for our twenty-fifth anniversary. It would be fantastic, but we lacked the staff to pull it off. So then the talk shifted to a concert. For the last three or four years, I had done a concert on Thanksgiving weekend in different churches in the Chattanooga area. The idea was for a special concert with May playing the piano and/or flute and Mima playing the piano and invite friends to be a part of it. Then the idea began to grow. I thought, *Why don't we put together an orchestra, a band, and a choir, and make this even bigger?* And then our plans grew larger. *Why not record this concert and turn it into a live concert DVD and Blu-ray?* It was a great idea but a very ambitious one. I shared it with my parents, and they were excited and supportive from the get-go. Having the support of my family gave me the courage to go after it!

One of the first people whose advice I sought was Sam Ocampo, my friend and mentor. In 1986, he had recorded a live album, *Friends,* which is one of my favorite albums. I was fortunate enough to be able to attend that concert and will never forget the several thousand people who were up on their feet throughout the concert as Sam played music that stirred the hearts and souls of everyone there. Sam knows so much about music, singers, songwriters, producers, labels, production, performance, and so forth, and I wanted his input. We've spent a lot of time together over the last few years. I played on the title song of his album *The Lighthouse;* he was present when I performed on the TV program *Hour of Power* with Dr. Robert Schuller at the Crystal Cathedral. We've had many performances together and have spent time devising marketing and sales strategies, not to mention countless unforgettable meals in fabulous restaurants.

I shared with him my initial idea for this event, and he advised me on a number of things, from the technical to the artistic. He even put me in touch with some of the finest people in the industry whom he knew and worked with: Michael Omartian, the legendary arranger and producer; Terry Christian, a top-notch recording engineer; and Paul Leim, a world-class drummer. Let me just say that I'm being quite modest by using these adjectives to describe these individuals! Their discographies and credit lists are jaw-dropping and eye-popping. Sam simply wanted me to be able to assemble the best musicians and participants I could get, so that the end product would be everything I hoped for.

When I was recording the album *Rock of Ages* in 2010 with John Stoddart, Sam did something I'll never forget. I hadn't recorded an album for more than four years. I was feeling rusty and unprepared. John's arrangements and performances were exquisite, and I just wasn't feeling up to par. Just before I began recording the violin solos, I called Sam one evening. I told him I was feeling insecure and overwhelmed. He was driving on Interstate 210 from Pasadena to Glendale, California, when I called him. Immediately, he perceived the angst in my voice, and he pulled over and stopped the car in order to talk and encourage me. He gave me a huge morale boost, and I felt much better! I'm honored to count Sam as one of my best friends, and I consider him a brother.

The second person I called was John Stoddart. There was no one else I had worked with more over the last several years, and I couldn't think of anyone else I felt more comfortable with to produce the musical part of this venture. He was on the same page with me, and he articulated and voiced ideas that were exactly what I wanted, even if I didn't realize it yet. Immediately we began to work on the list of songs, and John continued to tweak the list until we had the perfect list and order of songs as well as a wide variety of styles—classical, gospel, patriotic, jazzy, and so on. John is friends with, works with, and is the musical director for Kirk Whalum, the sax virtuoso, and immediately suggested I invite Kirk to be a guest musician on the album. There aren't enough accolades to describe Kirk's artistry, and soon I'd find out there weren't enough accolades to describe the human being that he is, either!

So with John on board, in addition to my family's support and Sam's help, it was time to present the idea before the Lord. Having undertaken the biggest recording project of my life in 1999, the *Christmas in the Aire* recording, I knew without a shadow of a doubt that without God's approval, blessing, and leading, anything I would attempt on my own was doomed to fail. Psalm 127:1 says, "Unless the LORD builds the house, they labor in vain who build it." As excited as I was about the prospect of this concert and recording, I wanted it to be God's will, not my will. This had to be God's project, not my project. It must be a celebration of twenty-five years of His ministry using me, not my twenty-five-year career celebration.

I knew that this project would require money—lots of it! The production of this album would easily cost in excess of one hundred thousand dollars. If this project was to take place, God would have to provide the resources. So I prayed and put the project before the Lord. I asked Him that if He wanted me to go forward, He would indicate His will by having the very first potential sponsor I contacted to be excited about coming on board.

With great exuberance as well as a stomach full of butterflies, I made an appointment to visit Beecher Hunter of LCCA. As I met with him and presented the project, the details, and what I thought was a mutually beneficial partnership, his face lit up with excitement. This was the indication I had sought from the Lord. When I left Beecher's office, I could barely contain myself. Of course, the work was only beginning, but knowing that God was in this, I knew we could not fail.

I knocked on several other doors, and many didn't open. But the Lord always provides what's needed!

Through what could only be God's leading, I was in Chicago doing concerts and called my friend Roger Cary, the chief operating office of Cancer Treatment Centers of America (CTCA), inviting him to have dinner with me. He happened to be home and had an evening free and graciously accepted. We dined at Froggy's Restaurant in Highwood, Illinois, close to his home; and as we caught up on our lives, I shared with him the project of the twenty-fifth anniversary concert and recording. Before I even asked him to consider CTCA's sponsorship, he suggested it. He saw potential for a great working relationship, and he jumped on board. Without CTCA's involvement, this project could not have become a reality. And its investment is proving to pay great dividends for all of us.

Thank you, Roger, for believing in me, this project, and my desire to serve the Lord—and for the opportunity for me to be a small part of the great work of Cancer Treatment Centers of America!

With John's help, I was able to secure the services of Michael Ripoll, guitarist, and Kelvin Wooten, bass player. These two young men are also top-notch musicians who routinely work with some of the most gifted (and well-known) artists of our time. John also put me in touch with Jason Max Ferdinand, the director of the Aeolians, an elite choir from Oakwood University in Huntsville, Alabama. Jason agreed to have the Aeolians be a part of this project. Michael referred me to Juan Carlos Santos, a Cuban-born percussionist, and I called on my friend Brian Taylor to be at the keyboards. I have known Brian since 2008 when I went to his church, the Church of the Redeemer in Gaithersburg, Maryland, for the first time. Brian served as the worship leader for this megachurch, and we became friends immediately.

Dr. Stephen W. Plate had hired me to be adjunct faculty at Gardner-Webb University in Boiling Springs, North Carolina, in 2000, and shortly after I moved to Cleveland, Tennessee, he was called to be the dean of the School of Music at Lee University in Cleveland. For this album, I asked him to conduct the orchestra, made up of talented young people from the area.

And of course, I asked my friend Dr. Frank González to be the master of ceremonies.

Our band was set:

- John Stoddart, musical director, arranger and coproducer
- Brian Taylor, keyboards
- Paul Leim, drums
- Juan Carlos Santos, percussion
- Michael Ripoll, guitar
- Kelvin Wooten, bass
- Stephen Plate, orchestra conductor
- Jason Max Ferdinand, choir director
- Aeolians, choir

If you Google these names, you'll find a mind-boggling list of credits and individuals that these incredibly talented musicians have worked with. Here's just a small sampling: Céline Dion, David Foster, Kenneth "Babyface" Edmonds, Barry Manilow, Andy Williams, Amy Grant, Conway Twitty, Dolly Parton, Eric Carmen, Doc Severinsen, George Jones, Kenny Rogers, Shania Twain, Willie Nelson, and on and on and on!

I also invited several other guest musicians and soloists to come and participate: my beloved mother, Mima; my sister, May; Sam Ocampo; Reinaldo Macías, a Cuban-born friend who lives in Chattanooga and who is a lyricist and opera star in Europe; my dear friend and recording artist, Jennifer LaMountain; gospel and jazz sax legend, Kirk Whalum; beloved singer and songwriter, Michael Card; and the incomparable Larnelle Harris.

My desire for this concert wasn't just to invite great musicians, but musicians who were dedicated to the Lord first and foremost, musicians and friends I had worked with before or whom I admired and desired to work with. To have these incredible artists be a part of this celebration was truly a dream come true!

I had invited other musicians, but due to previously scheduled concerts or time off to be with their families for Thanksgiving or other obstacles they weren't able to participate.

Without naming names, I want to share with you the challenges I had with the agent of one particular vocalist. I had seen her perform on TV shortly after my family arrived from Cuba in 1980. I really enjoyed this artist and was willing to pay her fee to have her come be a part of the project. So my friends Chauncey

Smith and Monique Roy, who've worked in the entertainment industry for many years, contacted her manager and agent. We found out all the particulars and requirements. Everything depended on whether a couple of the sponsors would come through. When they could not come on board, we contacted the manager and agent for this artist to let them know we would not be able to book the artist after all. The agent, who I'll call "Mr. Looney," tried to pressure us into signing the contract anyway. He called and e-mailed to tell us that the mere intent, interest, and inquiry on our part to book the artist were enough to legally bind us to use her. Of course, until one signs on the dotted line there's no deal. I guess he thought we'd been at this for twenty-five days instead of twenty-five years!

Nearly every week for a short period of time, we'd receive these harassing communications telling us we were on the hook and that we had to sign the contract. Marck Butler, the attorney who helped me with all the legal details of the concert, told me that the agent didn't have a leg to stand on. Every time I received an e-mail or phone call, I wanted to say, "Mr. Looney, you must be loony if you think we're buying your story." But I held my breath and tried to be professional about it. Eventually, he wanted us to sign a document saying that we had not signed a contract and that we would not be using the artist. Of course, we didn't sign anything because we had never signed anything to begin with!

Looking back, I can honestly say that only God's grace made it possible for us to undertake this project. There is no way I should have taken on this project. It was bigger than we could handle. But we had the biggest Guide, Protector, and Producer on our side—God Himself!

The two months leading up to the November 25, 2012, concert were two of the most trying and challenging months of my life. I did not slow down my concert schedule one bit. In October and November, I put on twenty-four concerts and several media performances and appearances in order to promote the twenty-fifth anniversary concert. I'd get on a plane Thursday or Friday, fly to wherever the concerts were that weekend, and come home Monday to keep working on the event. I worked eighteen to twenty hours a day the last two months! There were a couple of times that I felt I was at a breaking point. But five things got me through: (1) God; (2) the prayers of family and friends; (3) the loyal, constant, and invaluable help of our office manager, Kim Neal; (4) daily exercise; and (5) daily violin practice.

There were times I could sense that God was picking me up and carrying me. I had nothing in the tank, plans kept falling apart, obstacles were everywhere. But God was always with me. I'd get on my knees and ask Him to carry me, and He would!

There were also prayer warriors praying for us. At crucial times, I could feel these prayers of intercession. Sometimes I'd receive a phone call or a text from someone letting me know he or she was praying, and it would remind me of the fact that God was by my side.

Stretched to the limit herself, with too much on her plate, Kim Neal could tell how overwhelmed, feeble, and stressed I was at times. Over and over she'd ask me, "What's on your plate that you can't handle?" Or "What are you working on?" Or "Let me handle that." Then she'd add whatever it was to her responsibilities and take a huge burden off my shoulders. I am eternally grateful for the blessing that Kim is in my life. She is an amazing person, mother, and friend.

Exercising nearly every day provided an indispensable outlet for releasing stress and tension, and it gave me energy, clarity, and focus. No matter how exhausted I was, I ran every day. I did so for the obvious health benefits that exercise brings but also to discipline myself and to lose a few pounds. And practicing my violin allowed me to fall in love with the music on a regular basis. It also created an excitement in me as I thought about the night of the concert. It took my mind off all the work and helped me to see the light at the end of the tunnel.

In order to promote the concert and help sell out the venue, I played for a local ministerial association, appeared on a couple of local TV programs, and was interviewed for an article in the *Chattanooga Times Free Press*. People put up posters in area churches, Starbucks, community calendars, and spread the word in other ways. Deborah Gibbs, who is a very successful event promoter in the Chattanooga area, felt impressed to help out. She mobilized her vast list of contacts to get out the word. Deborah and I share the same hairdresser, Beth Guest, and at a chance meeting at the hair salon, we met and talked. By God's grace, all the tickets sold out!

Friends and concert attendees were coming from all over the country—from as far as Washington and California, and even outside the country. A friend from Brazil, Moacir Sena, an English professor, came with his wife all the way from São Paulo to attend the concert. We had planned a Thanksgiving meal to host some of these friends who were coming from so far. I am indebted to the many people who, upon arrival, saw the need for help and who spent part of the weekend carrying, lifting, transporting, and so on.

Several of my neighbors also became involved in a big way. My neighbor, Mary Ellen Ciganovich, formed a committee of five ladies—Mary Ellen as chair, Nancy Huston, Juanita Oliver, Andrea Boyd, and Kim Neal—to work on such things as locating a color guard for the patriotic medley; inviting local, state, and regional government officials; finding students in the area schools to serve as ushers at the concert; obtaining sponsorships for everything ranging from gift baskets for the guest musicians to television appearances and corporate investments; and a host of other details. Mary Ellen is a gifted speaker and author herself. She's faced huge physical disadvantages nearly her entire life and yet has managed to touch the lives of countless people through her presentations and her book. What an inspiration she is!

Glenn Hascall, who has worked as our publicist, sent out letters to many government officials around the country letting them know about our twenty-five-year celebration concert. Specifically, he wrote to President Barack Obama and former presidents George W. Bush, Bill Clinton, George H. W. Bush, and Jimmy Carter. I figured President Obama would be the only one who would respond. Who knows how many staff members the president has to respond to such requests (at the expense of the taxpayers), so I was fairly certain we would receive a letter of encouragement and/or congratulations from the current president. However, the only letter we received was from President George W. Bush. Say what you will about his policies, he took the time to write to someone he has never met, and will probably never meet, to congratulate us on twenty-five years of ministry for the Lord.

Family and friends began to arrive on Tuesday and Wednesday for the Thanksgiving holiday and the anniversary concert weekend. It was to be a memorable few days. To have my family with me, as well as so many friends who were able to make it, meant the world to me. Of course, there were some friends who absolutely couldn't make it. Two of those were Noel and Louise Garvin, who as my booking agents in Australia have traveled with me all over the country, scheduled many concerts for me, spent countless hours with me, and have helped bring Jesus to many. They wanted to come and tried everything humanly possible but just couldn't make it. But Noel and Louise, along with others, were there in spirit! We shared a beautiful Thanksgiving meal that so many helped prepare: Mima, May, Kim, Linda Hill, Dan and Dawn Heilbrun, my friend Keren Alonso, Don and Alice Merril, and others. Even with all the people eating Thanksgiving dinner with us, we still had food left over for almost a week!

We had one rehearsal Friday evening; the dress rehearsal was Saturday night; and the concert was Sunday night. When the rehearsal began and I heard the band playing, I was overcome with tears of joy. As we went through song after song, I thought of what each one meant to me personally and what I hoped it would do for every person at the concert and eventually for those watching the DVD or Blu-ray. "The Impossible Dream" reminded me of the power of dreaming big. The "Patriotic Medley" reminded me of how much I love this country. "Turn Your Eyes Upon Jesus" reminded me that all this was for the glory of God and His Son.

Weighing heavy on my heart was the fact that Sam Ocampo's father-in-law had fallen gravely ill that week. Sam and his wife, Gwen, had been scheduled to join us for Thanksgiving and the rest of the weekend. But on Monday, they had to fly to Southern California, along with the rest of Gwen's side of the family, for what appeared to be one last gathering of the family with her dad. As much as I missed the presence of Sam and Gwen, I wept for them losing her dad.

The day before the concert, I received a jolt of good news from Mima. She was checking Facebook on her mobile phone when she said, "Jaime, what happened to Sam?" I began to tell her that his father-in-law was very ill and that he and Gwen were not going to be able to make it. She then said to me, "He just checked in at Atlanta's Hartsfield-Jackson International Airport, according to Facebook." I could barely believe my ears! On Friday, Gwen's dad had rallied, and he was doing much better. When he was out of the danger zone, Sam got on a plane and flew all night in order to arrive twenty-four hours before the concert and be a part of it. I was grateful all the way around and had tears of joy when I heard the news!

I'm so very glad we put on a dress rehearsal performance Saturday night. There were so many little kinks that had to be worked out! Our set designer and associate producer, Edie Hughes, who has extensive experience with these kinds of events, brought all the heads together for a powwow after the dress rehearsal. It was late Saturday night, and everyone was exhausted. Even Keren, always willing to help out, came to the meeting with ideas. Sound, lighting, video, and stage people sat down to hammer out crucial details that needed fixing for Sunday night's performance. Thank God all this came to the surface, otherwise Sunday night might have been a ride through a minefield!

My best friend, Salim, flew down to be there for the dress rehearsal. We were able to spend a little time together after the concert. He had to fly out first thing the next morning and head to Brazil for a business meeting. My cousin Christine was able to come and stay until Saturday night as well. She returned to Pennsylvania and medical school the next morning.

Sunday afternoon, the Aeolians came, and along with Larnelle Harris and Michael Card, we went over several of the songs. Everything was now pretty much ready to go. Of course, everyone involved had ants in their pants running around, but things were in place. By the grace of God, all the hard work paid off.

I was too tired to be nervous! I was going on fumes, but the Lord sustained me. The concert and the evening were everything I dreamed—and then some. Walking out on to the stage and seeing a full house and feeling God's presence through the Holy Spirit was both exhilarating and calming at the same time. As I looked into the audience, I saw expressions of praise, joy, and delight. Seeing my mother sitting in the front row, enjoying the concert to the fullest, smiling and praising God, melted my heart! Seeing my father look at me with pride made me smile. Seeing my uncle enjoy the moment and music, seeing my sister getting into every song and note, brought me incredible happiness.

The most touching moments for me during the concert were (1) the trio with Mima and May, playing Mima's composition "My Plea, O Lord"; and (2) the tribute I gave to my parents after the song. A burning desire of mine has been, and is, to make my parents proud. Being able to do so for them that evening was an unforgettable experience.

Over and over, the audience responded to the music. The duets with Sam, Kirk, and Larnelle brought the house to their feet. The patriotic medley and the marching color guard brought goose bumps to even the termites on the pews! The trio with Mima and May was powerful and moving. My friends Jennifer and Reinaldo wowed the audience. John's arrangements and performance were masterful. And the finale, "Amazing Grace," was unforgettable. I began playing the first verse; the Aeolians then sang the first verse; and Michael made his way solemnly during the second verse. When Kirk played the third verse, I could not keep calm. His performance was spirited and powerful. Then Jennifer and Reinaldo sang the fourth verse with stirring pathos. By the time Larnelle was halfway through the fifth verse, everyone wanted to stand. Indeed, at the beginning of the sixth and final verse, when everyone sang and played, the crowd was standing, and there may not have been a dry eye in the audience.

When the song ended, there was a spontaneous burst of praise to God. I saw tears in the eyes of my friend Beecher Hunter, and it moved me to tears. My heart was pounding with joy and adoration. When we went into the reprise, I was so excited I don't think I knew what I was playing! If you pay close attention to the footage on the DVD, you'll see what I'm talking about! When we ended the reprise, I finished with an up bow, and I inadvertently leapt up.

As we came down from that spiritual high, Edie took to the stage for some brief words. Before the commencement of the concert, several friends had sent video greetings: Dr. Ben Carson; Bill Welte, executive director of America's Keswick, a Christian conference and retreat center; Pastor Joey Vazquez from Church of the Redeemer in Maryland; Pastor Karl Haffner from Kettering, Ohio; friend and pioneer, Max Mace, founder of the Heritage Singers; and others. My friend Dale Galusha, president of Pacific Press®, who had believed in this project, was there in person to offer support and congratulations. Sam presented a plaque from Max. I was humbled to receive all this warmth and love!

After the concert, a special moment for me was to see my family come together for the first time since 2008. That was the year my parents were divorced. But the Lord used that evening to mend fences and build bridges. Praise God!

Smallbox Entertainment Group, the video production company, did an amazing job of putting together the footage. Paul Kennamer Jr. is incredibly talented, and along with Merrilee Jacobs and the rest of the crew, created a documentary of the concert that is absolutely out of this world. I know you'll be blessed if you watch the DVD or Blu-ray.

Because of this concert and DVD, the Lord is opening new doors for ministry and witness. Cancer Treatment Centers of America is giving this DVD to pastors, patients, and staff. Sure, the DVD has a powerful segment that highlights the awesome outreach of CTCA. But the big picture is really all about Jesus. Invitations for performances and appearances in places I've never been before means opportunities to share Jesus with many people. Esperanza, an organization that has made, and is making, a powerful impact on the lives of many people, particularly Hispanics in this country, and led by a dedicated pastor and new friend, Luis Cortés Jr., has invited me to share at the National Hispanic Prayer Breakfast in Washington, D.C., on June 20, 2013, where hundreds of pastors and government leaders, including Barack Obama, the president of the United States, will be invited to attend. My prayer is that God will be glorified.

I wish I could capture and freeze what I felt and experienced at the end of the concert that night. I wanted to laugh. I wanted to cry. But mostly, I worshiped God. At that moment, I caught a glimpse, a small glimpse, of the depth and extravagance of God's amazing grace! We deserve nothing as sinners and human beings. But because God loves us so much, Jesus gave everything for you and me, and we are now sons and daughters of the King of the universe!

A full house.

At the studio in Pasadena, California, recording on Sam Ocampo's *The Lighthouse* CD.

With Sam Ocampo, John Stoddart, Kirk Whalum, Michael Card, and Larnelle Harris backstage before the concert began.

A duet with Kirk on "Sweet By and By."

John Stoddart and Jaime with Tony Campolo and Robert Schuller before the performace at the Crystal Cathedral.

My best friend Salim at the dress rehearsal.

The most touching moment of the concert for me—the trio with Mima and May.

My dad.

Playing with Larnelle Harris, Reinaldo Macías, Jennifer LaMountain, Kirk Whalum, and Michael Card during the finale song "Amazing Grace."

With May and friends Bob Norman and his wife, Jan, on the cruise to Alaska.

Ziplining with May in Alaska (Christian Edition 30th Anniversary Cruise, 2011).

With Dan and Dawn Heilbrun in Kona, Hawaii.

My friend Mark Newmyer.

GEORGE W. BUSH

November 9, 2012

Mr. Jaime Jorge
Ooltewah, Tennessee

Dear Jaime:

Congratulations on your 25th year in Christian music ministry.
People of faith have helped shape the culture and character of our
Nation by putting their beliefs and values into action. By
spreading God's message of boundless love and mercy, you help
lift hearts and make our country a more peaceful and hopeful
place.

Laura and I send our best wishes on this special occasion. May
God bless you, and may God bless our great Nation.

Sincerely,

George W. Bush

A letter from President George W. Bush.

CHAPTER 16

APPASSIONATO

{Passionately}

It was Friday evening, July 9, 2010. I had a weekend of concerts in the Washington, D.C., area. At the concert that night, as I shared what God had put in my heart to share with the congregation at the Capitol Hill Seventh-day Adventist Church, I tried to make eye contact with everyone, as I try to do at each concert. When the audience is large, that's sometimes difficult, if not impossible. But this night the church wasn't full by any means. At some point during the concert, I saw a pair of eyes looking up at me. My first thought was, *She is in pain!*

When the concert finished, I went to the lobby to greet people at the table as I do after every concert. Some artists don't enjoy interacting with people after the concert. I do. As I look at Jesus' ministry, most of His work began when He *finished* speaking. That's when people came to talk to Him, and He listened, He cried, He encouraged, and He healed. I've never healed anyone (that I know of), but I enjoy talking with people, sometimes praying with them, and interacting with folks who want to talk. The way I look at it, if people come out to hear me put on a two-hour concert, I can listen to those who want to come and share something with me afterwards.

So the young lady behind this pair of eyes came up to get a CD, and we said Hello. A number of folks lingered in the lobby, talking and catching up, and a little later I overheard a conversation near the table in which this young lady said that she was a vegan.

I was not completely vegan. I was giving vegan cooking classes and ate a mostly vegan diet plus fish. (Rachelle)

Now, I'm all about eating right, but I've never had the least bit of interest in being a vegan. Her words triggered in me the need to speak my mind! So I went over to the group and announced that I had never felt God's calling to be a vegan. She told me she was a cook and that she could make dishes you wouldn't even know were vegan. That piqued my interest, and I told her I'd like to try one of those dishes.

She sent me a couple of e-mails with recipes, and I gave them an honest-to-goodness effort. But it didn't work out. I'm an excellent cook myself. I'm hard to beat for anything that involves warming up in the microwave or on the stove for a few minutes! Beyond that, I won't win any Ultimate Chef contests nor do I have aspirations to be the next Chef Boyardee or Wolfgang Puck! I was dating someone at the time, so this was the extent of my communication with this young lady. What I didn't know was that she was going through a very painful divorce.

When I attended Jaime's concert at the Capitol Hill Church, I knew there was to be a musical event, but I had no idea who was playing. I just knew that I needed to be in church. As soon as I could get home from work, I hurried over to church, arriving after the concert had started. Jaime was right; I was in a great deal of pain. I was in the end stages of a divorce that I hadn't seen coming just nine months earlier. Despite my pain, I felt some peace that night as I was soothed and encouraged by the beautiful music Jaime played. I could see in him and feel in his music that he had a passion and love for the Lord. (Rachelle)

The next time we communicated was in December. She sent me an e-mail telling me what a blessing the CD she had purchased had been. I sent her a friend request on Facebook. We exchanged a couple of e-mails in January, and she told me she was going to visit her sister in Atlanta in February. I told her I didn't live too far from Atlanta and that perhaps we could meet for lunch. She gave me the dates she would be in Atlanta, and it worked out I was going to be home at that time. I looked at her Facebook profile to learn more about her and discovered that this girl was into sports—big time.

She had been a professional women's football player. And I'm not talking about the "lingerie league" either. This was the real deal! This was hard core. She was a running back; throughout her career, she had amassed quite an impressive set of stats: more than eleven thousand yards rushing in eleven years as a running back (and guys, the season consisted of eight games, not sixteen like in the National Football League), two-time Super Bowl champion, Super Bowl most valuable player, and so on. She had pictures on her Facebook page of her running over players from the opposite team as she ran to the end zone for a touchdown! I must say, I was a little apprehensive. What if I made her mad? Would she give me a stiff arm and run me over?

After she retired from football, she continued to be very active in sports, playing volleyball, running races, relays, half and full marathons, and so forth. As I pondered all this and our potential meeting on Friday morning, February 18, 2011, I figured that if I was to connect with her, I needed to meet her where she was. So I suggested that when we met that morning we should go for a run. She approved of the idea and also invited me to join her for a hot yoga class. I must say, I had never even heard of "hot" yoga. I thought yoga had something to do with meditation, so I wasn't so sure about this. I figured hot yoga must be done in a nice, warm room with some deep breathing. Boy, was I wrong!

That week I ran faithfully in my neighborhood every day, in order to get in shape. I have always loved sports, and there was a time when I was in great shape, playing a number of different sports—basketball, football, tennis, racquetball, and so on. But with my schedule being so crazy the last few years, I hadn't been very methodical about my workout routine. It had probably been three or four weeks since I last jogged or lifted weights. By Thursday, I was running a twelve-minute mile and feeling pretty good about it. I'm a fast-twitch muscle type, so I've never been big into or good at long distances. Speed and quickness were always my very good friends when I played sports.

My friend, Luis, who had come to do some maintenance at the house as well as updates and upgrades for a few weeks, accompanied me, and hung out elsewhere for the four or five hours Rachelle and I were going to spend together. He kept teasing me about being careful not to make her mad because she might tackle me hard!

I picked her up early Friday morning, and we went to a nearby park to run. Her pace was about an eight-minute mile, so from the very beginning, I had to play catch up. As we jogged, we talked. Rather, she talked. I gasped. She would rattle off a string of sentences like she on a stroll. I was timing my "Yes" and "No" answers in between sucking air so that I wouldn't seem to be so out of shape. We really had an interesting conversation, and I would remember more about it if my brain hadn't been so foggy from a lack of oxygen. I do remember being surprised at how many things we had in common. At one point I managed to run slightly ahead of her and turn and ask, "Are you the female version of Jaime Jorge?"

I remember that moment so vividly that I could tell you to this day exactly where we were on the running trail (on the far side of the loop, running up a slight incline), the look on Jaime's face when he asked me that question (pleasantly puzzled, as if I were an anomaly), and on which side of me he was running (the right side). In that moment I was struck by how much we truly did have in common—and pleasantly surprised by it. (Rachelle)

As we approached the end of the third mile—it seemed to me more like the ninth mile—she said, "I'm feeling energetic; do you want to go another mile?"

I quickly responded, "I would love to, but I *really* don't want to miss our hot yoga class or have to rush around when we get there." I tried to sound genuine and mindful of our schedule. She bought it, or at least she never said anything to the contrary.

> *Yep, I bought it—hook, line, and sinker! Throughout the run, I did not realize that Jaime was struggling to keep up with me as much as he says. He gave a valiant performance! I was under the impression that he was a regular runner; before we ran together, I wondered if he would outpace me. I had been distance running just a little over a year, and like Jaime, I was a natural sprinter and fast-twitch muscle fiber athlete. (Rachelle)*

When we arrived at the yoga studio, I looked around to see what the protocol was for preparation, setting up, and so on. Since it was winter, the room felt nice and toasty. Well, it didn't take long before I was being boiled alive. The next ninety minutes were going to be a battle to survive the class! The instructor began giving instructions, and ten minutes into the class, I was feeling light-headed. We had done these breathing exercises, and I had taken in too much oxygen. But I knew there was no way I could walk out of the class now.

As the minutes inched by, perspiration was jumping out of my body like a gymnast jumps off a trampoline. I could hear my heart racing, and I kept my mouth closed in case my heart decided to jump up and out through my throat because of the workout I was giving it. Every once in a while, in between postures, I'd look at Rachelle to see if she was even acknowledging my superhuman, herculean effort. But no, she was focused squarely on her postures, sweat pouring from her body, too, not even appreciating my great sacrifice.

> *What Jaime didn't know about me is that once in the zone, I am totally focused on what I'm doing. The athlete in me blocks out all distractions to focus on successful completion of the goal. Even so, I would occasionally take a peek to see how he was doing. I always do that when I introduce someone new to hot yoga, so I can gauge whether they will come to a second class. Jaime must have been focusing on not passing out each time I glanced his way to check on him! (Rachelle)*

I couldn't understand what the instructor was saying. It was enough just to focus on not fainting, telling myself to breathe, and assuring myself that I was going to live through this martyrdom. I watched everyone around me and tried to do what they were doing. There was a moment during the class, probably about seventy minutes in, that I thought I saw the heavens open up. But it was just a bit of steam rising from this room that was at 110 degrees Fahrenheit and 65 percent humidity. But I told myself I'd rather be carried out of there on a stretcher, or be dead, than walk out of the class.

For ninety minutes, I was in that torture chamber, stretching muscles I didn't know existed, and contorting my body as if I were in a DuPont lab abusing rubber. I don't know how I made it through the class. Part of it was anger at whoever invented this madness, and the other part was fear that I'd walk out of the class before it ended and Rachelle would think me to be a wuss! All I know is that when I came out of there, I had never been so happy to walk out into winter. I went upstairs to take a shower and try to regather all the marbles into my brain, because I think they had all run away like the Road Runner evading Wile E. Coyote! I took a cold shower that seemed to me like manna from heaven for a starving man.

I managed to compose myself and meet Rachelle downstairs to go have lunch. I was so hungry after a three-mile sprint and a ninety-minute debacle that I even accepted when she suggested we go to a vegan health-food store and café across the street. I hadn't heard of many of the dishes, plates, vegetables, and healthy ingredients in those menu items. But when I found something that included the word *avocado,* I knew I had been saved by the bell, and I ordered whatever that item was. Rachelle suggested I try a drink called "kombucha," and I did. I was so dehydrated I could have gone to the nearest swimming pool to drink that down. I had four bottles of water before I replenished enough fluids in my body to go to the restroom.

It was during that early lunch conversation that I was really taken with Rachelle. We shared a meaningful conversation about our lives, our highs, our lows, and so on. This is when she told me that her divorce had been finalized four months after I met her in Washington, D.C., which was the same month the girl I had been seeing ended our relationship. She told me how devastatingly painful her divorce had been, and I shared with her how I definitely understood and could relate to that. There was even a moment, I thought, when there was a spark in her eyes as we looked at each other. I had to drive back to Chattanooga with Luis, because I had a plane to catch that afternoon for Dallas/Fort Worth where I had several concerts that weekend.

Before we said Goodbye, I felt the urge to tell her that I really wanted to get to know her better as a friend. But I withstood the urge to open my mouth. We exchanged a few other pleasantries, and I left. On the way back to Chattanooga, Luis wanted to know if she had run circles around me during our jog, if she had run me over yet, or if I thought I could ever keep up with her. I was definitely drawn to her, but I certainly didn't see myself going back to hot yoga, much less turning vegan or running marathons just to be with her.

During those short hours we spent together, I really enjoyed myself. I instantly felt comfortable around Jaime. He was very engaging, making me laugh often. We never lacked for interesting conversation. I had the sense that we could talk indefinitely without running out of things to say. During our lunch conversation, Jaime sat back, shrewdly appraising me, and said "You are a completely different person than the woman I met in July. Your eyes have so much more life in them." When I asked him to elaborate, he told me that when we had first met, I seemed wilted and withdrawn and that he thought perhaps I was shy. (I think I almost spit out my food trying not to laugh, because anyone who knows me will tell you they wouldn't use these words to describe me.) It was then that I cautiously shared with Jaime some of the pain I had experienced going through my divorce. He was empathetic in his response, and I knew it was genuine. I also sensed a peace within him that I had not seen before in many people, and that was very appealing.

When he dropped me off at my sister Chandra's house, she wanted the scoop right away. "Well," she said, "how did it go? Are you interested in him romantically?"

With a confused expression on my face, I responded, "I'm not sure. It looks really good on paper."

She raised her eyebrows as she said, "You're going to need more than a good-looking piece of paper." I knew that I was intrigued by this man and that we matched up on all of the things we had discussed, but at that moment I did not seem to be able to process the step that a woman takes when, in her mind, she changes a man's status from possible friend to possible romantic interest. I know some of it had to do with the fact that I had just started thinking about dating again and was feeling really overwhelmed by the process. I think that if Jaime would have spoken, instead of squashing his instinct, and told me what he wanted to say about developing a real friendship, I would have been willing and able to take that ball and run with it. (Rachelle)

We exchanged a few texts after that, and it was the end. Every once in a while I'd check out her Facebook page and even leave a comment. But for the most part, that was the extent of our communication or interaction—until late August 2012.

I was on vacation in Hawaii with my close friends Dan and Dawn Heilbrun, who are from Washington. I had met them at a concert in their church in Puyallup in 2005, and they had volunteered to help me at the table. They set up, tore down, and even invited me for lunch. That was the beginning of a friendship that has grown beautifully over the last few years. We have shared several trips to Hawaii for concerts followed by a little rest and relaxation. Countless times Dan and Dawn have accompanied me to concerts and helped me; my home away from home in Washington State is with them!

One afternoon, as Dan, Dawn, and I were relaxing in the condo in Hawaii,

I sat down to glance at Facebook and saw Rachelle's profile picture: she was at a beach. I went to her page and noticed that she was on vacation with her sister in Puerto Rico. Her profile picture was of the standing bow yoga posture at the edge of a waterfall. I decided to send her a text. It went something like this: "Hi Rachelle, it's Jaime. Looks like you're in paradise! Well, so am I. Hope you're having a great time." I was hoping she'd text back and inquire where I was. She did text back, acknowledging my text, but she didn't ask me where I was. It took her a few hours to text me back. This would become a regular pattern: I'd text her, and two or three hours later (or two or three *days* later), she'd respond. It made me so exasperated (code word here for mad) that sometimes I'd set the alarm on my iPhone to respond to her text in the exact amount of time it took her to respond to me, down to the minute! Of course, she never noticed it or mentioned it.

> *Much later, when Jaime told me he had actually set an alarm to make me wait the same amount of time for a text response as he had waited for mine, I burst into laughter. I thought it was hilarious that he would "punish" me that way, and I never even knew it! I do remember that I was pleased to hear from him. I never imagined that by the end of the year I would be falling in love with him and that less than one year later, we would be married. (Rachelle)*

After a few very distant and diplomatic texts, all of a sudden I was surprised by her next one. It said something like, "Jaime, can I ask you for a favor? I would like to solicit your prayers. I'm going through a difficult time right now. And please let me know how I can pray for you."

That was quite a surprise, given the tone of our text conversations thus far. She didn't tell me what was wrong, and I didn't ask. But I take prayer and prayer requests very seriously, so I began to pray for her daily. Once or twice a week I'd text her to see how she was doing, and she'd usually tell me that she was struggling. As it turned out, while she was in Puerto Rico, she and her boyfriend broke up, and things went back and forth for the next few weeks. As the old Neil Sedaka song says, "Breaking up is hard to do," and she was going through the difficult and painful experience of a breakup. Once in a while, I'd pray for her and in order to encourage her, I'd text her my prayer. She would often respond that she was very encouraged by these prayer texts.

> *When I would receive those prayer texts from Jaime, I was always very encouraged by them. It was a huge help to know that I had prayer warrior friends interceding for me. After receiving one of the prayer texts, I remember asking him, "Does this count as 'two or more gathered together' to give us more power in prayer?" His response: "Absolutely!" (Rachelle)*

It just so happened that I was going to have some concerts in the Washington, D.C., area the weekend of November 9–11, so I asked Rachelle if she wanted to get together and (as you might imagine) go for a run and then go to a hot yoga class. I figured that would make her feel comfortable, and besides, it would be better that than having to eat at a vegan restaurant! She agreed, and additionally she told me that she and possibly her mom would like to attend one of the concerts. She invited me to have brunch after the run and yoga before the late afternoon concert. I was beginning to get excited about having a little time to share with her and get to know her better, when she totally deflated and burst my bubble. About ten days before I was to go to D.C. for the weekend, she called me to go over some things pertaining to the schedule of activities for that weekend and asked me if it would be all right if a group of ladies from her church were a part of the run.

That hit me like a ton of bricks! I thought to myself, *She's trying to create enough distance here so that she won't have to allow me any kind of a window to learn about her and know her better.* I put on a brave voice and told her that, sure, it would be excellent, and the ladies were most welcome to join us on the jog. But when I got off the phone, I was mad! I went to talk to Kim, whom I've come to rely on and trust so much. I told her what Rachelle had just said and that I thought it was a tactic on her part and I would have none of it. I told Kim I'd just wait until a couple of days before we were to get together, and then tell her that my schedule had gotten crazy and I wouldn't be able to make it. I certainly had enough of an excuse in that I needed to spend that time practicing the violin for the concert just two weeks later, instead of going out for a run with a group of ladies.

Immediately after I finished talking, Kim said to me, "You know that if you cancel on her, that'll be the end of any possibility to get to know her." I knew she was right, but I was still burning from what Rachelle had just done—at least the way I interpreted her actions. And I was fairly justified in thinking that way, for until that point, she had been very distant and careful with me. As it turned out, she had recently been chosen to lead the health ministry of her church, and she was trying to start a program where, one day every week, the ladies of the church would gather to run. Unlucky for me, the day we were to get together was the day the whole group was to run!

Early Sunday morning I met Rachelle and the ladies from the group to run. It was a chilly morning in D.C., and we ended up running pretty much by ourselves since our pace put us ahead of the group. We ran past the Capitol to the Washington Monument and back. It was about five miles. Afterward, we went to the Capitol Hill Bikram Yoga studio where Rachelle attends class regularly. Although my second experience with hot yoga was just as traumatizing as the first, this time I knew what I was in for. So I took lots of water to keep hydrated. When the class ended, I showered upstairs, and Rachelle went home to get ready, bring her mom, and meet me at the place she had chosen to have brunch—a French restaurant called Montmartre in the Eastern Market part of D.C.

It didn't take me long to get to the restaurant. I was excited and a little nervous. She and her mom seemed to take forever to get there. Finally, we sat down. I had a great time. The conversation was fluid and comfortable, especially with her mom. Rachelle was affable, but she was not giving me much to go on. I was trying to see if she had some kind of affinity for me. I know that she was nursing a broken heart, but I was hoping to see if there was *any* interest on her part!

> *I really enjoyed spending time with Jaime that morning and afternoon. Once again, he was easy to be around, and we had a great conversation on our run. Even so, I did not think I was in a position to be romanced, so I did try to keep some distance. At that point I was not sure if he was interested in me as a friend or possibly had romantic interest, so I asked my mom to pay close attention and tell me what she thought. If he was interested in something more than friendship, I wanted to hit the brakes! (Rachelle)*

I had to rush the end of brunch a bit in order to be on my way for the 4:00 P.M. concert in Beltsville, Maryland. Rachelle and her mom were going to attend, along with her younger sister, Stephanie, and good friend Paula Jackson. As it turned out, the concert was at 4:30, not 4:00 as I had thought. So I texted her and told her she didn't need to rush to get to the church. That was the second time that weekend that I had gotten the time of a concert wrong. I texted her to tell her that I was a bit of a mess that weekend, but that at least I had gotten the time of our early morning run right. Her response? "You managed to show up on time to the one activity that could've started without you." *Ouch!* I told you she wasn't giving me much!

The church wasn't packed by any means, but the Lord really blessed the concert. It was a benefit concert for a Filipino congregation in the area, and several thousand dollars were raised that late afternoon and early evening. And the spiritual blessings were bountiful! Many hearts were touched, and people were inspired to serve the Lord. As I looked around the audience while sharing some testimonies, I kept an eye on Rachelle. When I looked at her, she wasn't looking at me. For the life of me, I couldn't get a read on this girl!

> *Before the concert began, Jaime came over to our seats and greeted us. I introduced him to Paula and my sister, Stephanie, and we all chatted for a few minutes. As soon as we finished talking, I suddenly became very hot and had to take off my jacket. As the concert progressed, I alternated between being cold and hot and kept taking my jacket off and putting it back on. I turned to Paula, saying, "Is it hot? Are you hot? I think it's hot in here!" After I had done this several times, Paula leaned back, crossed her arms, and with an amused smirk on her face,*

said, "I'm liking this!" Before I had any idea, Paula knew that Jaime and I had potential. (Rachelle)

After the concert was over, I went to the table to greet people and sign the CDs, DVDs, books, T-shirts, and so on that people asked to have autographed. Rachelle and her family and friends hovered about, and I tried to make sure I knew where they were, hoping they wouldn't just leave. It wasn't easy, as there was a great deal of enthusiasm at and around the table, and I had lots to do. Filipinos are warm, friendly, and musical; they treated me like family. It was pandemonium at the table as people were eager to obtain our resources.

I had been invited to go to a small reception following the concert, but an unexpected personal situation arose that I had to take care of, and I wasn't able to go. After that, Rachelle came up to me and told me she and her mom would like to invite me to dinner. Inside, I jumped up and down and did the wave. Outside, I calmly smiled and said, "I'd love to!" There's a pretty good Cuban restaurant in Silver Spring, Maryland, called Cubano's, and I suggested we go there. I wanted them to try the food I grew up on.

After the concert, Jaime was very busy at the table, and I didn't want to interrupt him. I could see that everyone was so excited to speak with him, and I didn't think I should monopolize his time. After all, I had already spent quite a bit of time with him that day. I also didn't want to just leave without thanking him for a beautiful concert, and all of us wanted to purchase some CDs. So, my mom, Stephanie, Paula, and I spent some time talking. After things calmed down at the table, we made our way over so we could make our purchases and thank Jaime. Stephanie and Paula had to leave after that, and my mom and I had plans to go out to dinner together (she still owed me a very belated birthday dinner). As we discussed our dinner plans, I asked my mom if she thought we should invite Jaime. I figured that he would appreciate some company for dinner since he was traveling alone. Mom thought it was a fantastic idea! (Rachelle)

As I drove to the restaurant, I was bursting with anticipation. I also remember praying and asking God to open all the right doors and close all the wrong ones. We got out of our cars and met inside the restaurant. Rachelle sat to my left, and her mom across from us. A painted wall was to her left. We had a fantastic time talking and trying several different appetizers (*mariquitas,* which are long slices of fried plantains; *yuca frita,* which is a white, fibrous, and tubular root also known as cassava; and *maduros,* which are sweet plantains), salads and our different main course dishes. At one point, I took one of these long, curly, thin *mariquitas* and went to feed it to Rachelle. She promptly took it from my hand and fed it to herself. *Thank you very much,* I thought to myself.

> *Now, every time I think of the moment Jaime tried to feed me the* mariquita, *I laugh out loud. Although at that moment, I was almost horrified because I didn't expect it. As far as I was concerned, I was having dinner with a friend and my mom. I remember thinking,* Does he think this is a date? Because it's not a date! But he just tried to feed me something, so maybe he thinks it's a date. But it can't be a date, because we didn't say it was a date—and my mom is here! *(Rachelle)*

From what I remember, I was having a fantastic conversation with her mom! I don't think Rachelle turned to look at me three times during the entire dinner. She was definitely into the conversation, but our body languages were worlds apart! I was dialed in, and she seemed like she was standing with a stiff arm ready for me. Nevertheless, I was encouraged. They—she—*had* invited me to dinner. That *must* mean something, right? Rachelle tells me that after we said goodbye and she and her mom got in her car to drive back home, her mother said to her, "Honey, you're in trouble." Of course, I didn't know any of this. But I told myself the same thing: "Jaime, you're in trouble!"

> *As I started the car and we buckled our seat belts, I turned to Mom and said, "Never mind what I asked you earlier about letting me know if you think Jaime is interested in me as more than a friend. I think I can figure this one out without any assistance." (Rachelle)*

As we went our separate ways following dinner, I didn't want the evening to end. I was exhausted after a five-mile run, a ninety-minute hot yoga torture session, *and* a concert. But my mind was racing! Then I noticed that the water bottle and towel Rachelle had lent me that morning were still in my car. Looking for any excuse to see her again, I quickly rang her on her mobile phone and told her that I would be happy to drive back down to D.C. to give her these "precious" belongings. But she said they were disposable, and not to worry about it. Well, at least I tried!

The next morning, Monday, November 12, I had a presentation in nearby Columbia, Maryland, before heading to Baltimore-Washington International Airport to catch my flight home. I was still pretty tired, but I couldn't stop thinking about Rachelle. When I arrived home in Ooltewah that evening, I phoned her for a brief call. I told her that I didn't know where she stood or what she thought of me, but that I was going to pursue her until she told me to go away. I think I caught her off guard because she didn't say much. "*Um,* OK," was her response. At least she had been warned!

Jaime definitely surprised me when he told me that. I wasn't sure what to do with that or what to do with him. I knew I liked him as a friend. I enjoyed being around him, and he was a really amazing person. I also knew, or thought I knew, that I wasn't in a position to explore the possibility of a romance with him. (Rachelle)

There was one really good thing, which in retrospect, was providential—she had already made plans to visit her sister Chandra and her family in Atlanta for the Thanksgiving weekend, so I invited her to come to the twenty-fifth anniversary concert on November 25, which would give us another opportunity to see each other. So every night until that weekend, we spent a few minutes talking. Neither of us had a lot of time, as she was busy with several work projects, and I was working around the clock in preparation for the concert, but we managed to talk and pray every night.

Most of the concert's guests and participants were staying at the same hotel, so Rachelle came in late Saturday night, November 24, and checked into her room. I was still at the church after the dress rehearsal, but finally, around midnight, I made my way to the hotel lobby where we spent a few minutes chatting. Of course, it took a while to actually sit down with her, because my friend Mark Newmyer was there with friends and family, and we spent a few minutes talking. Eventually, Rachelle and I sat down to talk. She said she had had a beautiful Thanksgiving with her sister and family, but then she told me that she was going through a bit of a difficult moment. And as was our custom, we prayed for God's intervention and leading. When we opened our eyes, we looked at each other at the same time. It was a powerful moment; I felt the earth shake under me right when our eyes met.

It was a powerful moment, indeed! When our eyes locked at the end of that prayer, it felt like a high volt electric current passed through my body. We both quickly looked away. I think we were surprised by the moment and a bit unnerved by it. (Rachelle)

By now, it was about 1:30 A.M., and by the time I got to sleep another hour had passed. I was going on fumes, but I didn't feel it at that point. Early Sunday morning Rachelle drove up to the house so that we could—guess what—go for a run! If you run the entire length of the paved road of my neighborhood, it's almost four and a half miles. But there are a lot of hills. Even though Rachelle was in much better shape than I was, I was accustomed to the hills, some of which are at a forty-degree angle. It was the closest I had come yet to giving her a run for her money! But at least there is no hot yoga in Chattanooga, so I was not going to have to do that. Yippee!

After the run, we came back to the house, where she spent a bit of time with

Mima and my sister Maydelé. This was a crucial moment, because what Mima and May think and say is very important to me! And my sis is very honest with me and very protective. I went to take a shower to get ready to head to the church. Rachelle sat down to talk to Mima and May. After I came out of the shower, May came up to me and said, "I really like this girl!" That was *very good*! Later, Mima told me she absolutely loved Rachelle and that they had spent quite a bit of time talking and sharing.

Before I got in the car, Rachelle came to the garage and offered a prayer for me. It brought me peace and allowed me to relax. It was also the first time we had held hands—even if just during prayer, this was good!

Halfway through the afternoon, Rachelle came to the church to pick up her tickets for the concert. Her mom, Mary, her youngest sister, Marina, and her nephew, Colin, would be joining her for the concert. She gave me a lovely card of encouragement, which I opened just before the concert began. It brought me joy. The next time I saw her was right before the last song. The auditorium part of the church was pretty dark in order to give the video cameras all the focus and light they needed to capture what was going on up front on the stage. So it wasn't easy to see the audience, but I tried to make eye contact with the crowd and also to spot Rachelle. I couldn't see her anywhere. I wondered if something had happened. But at last, I saw her and was able to set my mind at ease.

After the concert, I greeted people and took pictures. Eventually, I was able to come over to where Rachelle was with her mom, sister, and nephew. It was a bit of an awkward moment. She looked stunningly beautiful, and I wanted to tell her so. But her mom and family were there, and I didn't want to make her uncomfortable, as I didn't know what she had told them about my (or her) interest level. Also, my previous experience had been that every time I had complimented her, or tried to, she had rebuked me. So I gave everyone a hug, exchanged a few pleasantries, and said, "I'll see you tomorrow." Well, as you might imagine, that didn't go over very well!

Jaime is right; it was *an awkward moment, for several reasons. First, once the concert ended, we were some of the last people still in our seats, as we waited for him to greet us. We didn't want to leave without thanking him for the tickets or before I could introduce him to my sister and nephew. They had both really enjoyed the concert and wanted to meet Jaime. By the time he was able to make his way over, the place was almost empty. Second, before the concert, Jaime had asked me to pay attention to how each song made me feel and what I really thought about each one, so that I could share those thoughts and feelings with him the next day when we planned to get together for a run and lunch. He asked me to give him raw and honest feedback. Well, when someone asks me something like that, I take it very seriously. So, during the concert, after each song, I wrote notes on my program so I wouldn't forget anything when I shared it with him the next day. What I hadn't anticipated was that by doing this I became very emotionally invested in the concert and in the moment, which left me feeling quite vulnerable. It was an incredible experience, and I am so glad I was there to see and feel God moving in such a powerful way through all of the talented musicians who were a part of the concert. Third, on top of that, it was during this concert that I first allowed myself to realize that I was really starting to care about Jaime—quite possibly as much more than a friend. Fourth, Jaime's brief (and awkward) greeting was confusing to me in light of how he had previously interacted with me. Fifth, before the concert started, I prayed and asked God to work in my life and my heart that evening, to answer some questions that I had about some difficult things I was dealing with at the time. He did, and with all of those things combined, that entire day hit me like a ton of bricks. (Rachelle)*

The next morning I called her at the hotel to coordinate when we'd get together for a run and breakfast. As soon as she answered, I could tell something was wrong. "Is everything OK?" I asked.

"I'm in a bit of a funk this morning," she replied.

I asked when she wanted to get together, and she told me she was doing a bit of work and that we could meet when she was finished. This was the last day I was going to be home before heading out on a Christmas tour of thirty-one concerts in twenty-eight days, so I had plenty to do.

Soon I picked her up, and we found a place to run. (She didn't want to run in my neighborhood again!) Then I took her back to the hotel so she could shower and get ready to check out of her room. I went home to take a shower and come back to pick her up for lunch. We went to Jason's Deli in the Hamilton Place Mall area in Chattanooga. After lunch, we went to Starbucks to sit down and talk some more. It was there that we had a pretty definitive conversation.

At some point, I said, "I have been a failure at my previous relationships, and I don't want to keep making the same mistakes over and over again. Instead of jumping into a relationship, then finding out things just aren't working, and having to back out, which is painful, uncomfortable, and difficult, I want to do things differently. I have a set of questions for you. If the answers are right, then let's proceed. If not, then let's just be friends." This may sound a bit haughty, but it really wasn't meant that way. And she understood.

"As a matter of fact," she said to me, "I have a set of questions for you too!" And so we began. Here are the first few questions I asked:

1. What is your credit score? (If a girl doesn't know how to be organized, responsible, and punctual, it won't work for me.)

2. What is your relationship with God like, and how important is it to you? (If God isn't the top priority, it won't work.)
3. How is your relationship with your family? (I want someone who is close to her family.)
4. What is your relationship like with your dad? (Girls whose fathers don't have a strong, meaningful, loving relationship and presence in the lives of their daughters have an uphill battle to climb later on when getting into relationships.)
5. What are your goals in life? (A girl who is dependent, who isn't driven or motivated, or who is expecting an easy ride, isn't going to be compatible with me.)

On I went with the rest of my questions. To my great joy, everything Rachelle said matched exactly what I wanted and needed to hear. So my examination was over. Now it was her turn. When I answered her questions satisfactorily, we knew we were on to something.

It was really incredible how we matched in every area with our responses! We covered all of the topics that usually take months of dating to address, and we still hadn't actually been on a date (or so I thought). We spent hours talking that day. The only thing that ended our time together was the fact that he had a thirty-one-day tour to pack for and I had borrowed my sister's car and needed to get it back to her. (Rachelle)

Before she returned to Atlanta that evening, we prayed. We asked the Lord to guide our friendship and to open doors and bless it if this relationship was of His doing. And if it wasn't, we asked Him to close doors. We put ourselves in His hands. And there's no better place to be than in God's hands!

Rachelle in action.

Rachelle was a running back, linebacker, and punter for the Delaware Griffins, 2004.

CHAPTER 17

FORTISSIMO
{Very Loud}

I left on Tuesday, November 27, for Toronto, Canada, for the start of the Christ-mas concert tour. I would not return home until after Christmas. From that point on, Rachelle and I talked on the phone or communicated via Skype or FaceTime every single day, sometimes for several hours. I don't know how we did it. She was very busy at work, and I was giving concerts every single day or night, except for Mondays, which is when I traveled to the next destination. I was going on fumes, but something was growing inside me that was giving me energy and strength. During the next ten days, we talked on more than one occasion until four or five in the morning, and I had to get up at six!

> *We learned so much about each other in that week. In looking back, I joke that we did about seven months of dating in the first two weeks of talking daily, because we covered so much ground. I was still reticent about considering anything more than friendship, and yet I knew that every time Jaime and I talked, I felt a peace unlike anything I had ever before experienced in interaction with another human being. I was physically, mentally, and emotionally exhausted, and yet I had an energy that I could not explain. (Rachelle)*

I had eight performances in Ontario from November 27 to December 2. On Monday morning, December 3, I went to the studios of Crossroads Christian

Communications in Burlington, Ontario, to tape programming for their Christmas broadcasts on *100 Huntley Street,* which is the most popular Christian TV program in Canada. I've had the privilege of being invited to appear on *100 Huntley Street* several times over the years, and it is always a pleasure to return. From there, I flew to Miami, spent the night at my uncle Leonel's house in Miami Beach, and then flew to San Salvador, El Salvador, to share at the Latin American Mission Conference of the Baptist Missionary Association of America. It was a spiritual high to be a part of this conference, meet the dedicated missionaries who have left comfort and security to bring salvation to countless people, and encourage them through music and testimony. The head of the department for Latin America is Brother Phil Knott, an indefatigable traveler and dedicated servant of the Lord, who is also my friend.

At the hotel, I changed rooms twice in my quest for a strong Wi-Fi signal, so that any time Rachelle was available, we could get together on FaceTime. If you don't know, FaceTime is a feature of the iPhone that allows you to videoconference with anyone, as long as you're both connected to the Internet via Wi-Fi. What a blessing this technological feature is! And what a fabulous technological wonder the iPhone is! Rachelle and I looked forward to spending this time together with great anticipation. At the end of each conversation, we always prayed. And we were so tired, and our prayers so long, that on more than one occasion, one of us fell asleep while praying!

From El Salvador, I flew to Philadelphia for five concerts in New Jersey, New York, and Pennsylvania. Since D.C. isn't too far from Philadelphia, and Rachelle's mom lives in Chambersburg, Pennsylvania, Rachelle planned on coming to spend time with me during the weekend. At first, I was not excited about the idea because when you have five presentations in forty-eight hours, that leaves little to no time to spend with someone. But she had made up her mind, and I wasn't going to try to dissuade her.

Jaime told me he wasn't sure it was a good weekend for me to visit with him, because his time was so packed with concerts and travel. What he didn't know is that I thought this was the perfect reason for me to go. I wanted to see what Jaime's life was like on the road, and in looking at his concert schedule, I saw there wasn't another opportunity for me to do so for several months. At this point, I had seen only three of his concerts, and I was curious as to what an entire weekend of concerts would entail and how different my perspective would be with a behind-the-scenes glimpse of things. I have always believed that a good way to get to know someone quickly is to see that person in action, doing the things he does most often. I figured that five concerts in two and a half days would have to involve excellent time management and likely produce a potentially stressful situation or two. I have learned that how a person behaves under stress is the best indicator of how they will respond in future stressful or difficult circumstances. I wanted to know if this guy was as easygoing and positive under duress as he was in other situations. On the phone, it's much easier to mask a negative reaction than it is in person. And so far, most of our time spent together was on the phone. I wasn't interested in Jaime Jorge the performer. I wanted to know and understand the live version of Jaime Jorge! (Rachelle)

The first concert was on Friday night in Laurelwood, New Jersey. We had supper before the concert at the home of Bill and Catherine Schofield. I met them several years ago when I went to that area; now whenever I have concerts around there, I stay with them.

I couldn't help but laugh at the stark contrast between my last concert in the United States and this one. At my last American concert, just a week and a half earlier, the church had been packed, tickets had run out, and excitement and enthusiasm had pulsated everywhere. For whatever reason, the present concert was not well attended, and I quipped to Rachelle that this is the life of a musician, and asked her if she was sure she was OK with it. She said that wasn't an issue with her.

Something really impressed me about her: that night, as the table was set up, she took notice of all the details—how the CDs, DVDs, and books were placed, how we interacted with people, talked to them, prayed with them, helped them, and so on. From that point on, Rachelle took over all those details at the concerts. She handled the table as if she had been doing it for years! I was amazed. With the people, she was engaging, warm, and friendly; she didn't get frazzled when there was a bit of a mob scene with people wanting the products.

I immediately felt right at home doing these things. It was as if I had been there all along, sharing in this inspiring ministry. I loved meeting the people that attended that concerts and was humbled that they would feel comfortable enough to ask me to pray for and with them. (Rachelle)

The next concert after Laurelwood, New Jersey, was at the Old Westbury Seventh-day Adventist Church in New York. One of the members of that church, Tony DeFranco, had made a contribution twenty-five years earlier to help me buy my violin. I was overcome with emotion as I acknowledged and thanked him for believing in me when I was just seventeen years old.

From there, I went to Liberty Corner, New Jersey, where I met Rachelle, her mom, Mary, and her youngest sister, Marina, for the concert at Fellowship Deaconry. This was the same place where I had arrived for a concert eight and half years earlier without my violin. But this time, it was with me!

I was nervous because I planned on talking to Mary that night to tell her that I was very serious about her daughter. I wanted to assure her that I had nothing but the best of intentions in seeking a friendship, courtship, and relationship with Rachelle.

This was my third time to play at Fellowship Deaconry, and several of those attending had been to every presentation. During the concert, I introduced Rachelle, Mary, and Marina, and I shared with the audience a little of our story. Everyone was absolutely delighted! I dedicated a piece to Rachelle, the Italian aria "'O Sole Mio." When I finished, the audience burst into applause, and when I looked at Rachelle, she had her hand on her heart and had had it there during the whole piece, without realizing it.

> When Jaime announced that he was dedicating "'O Sole Mio" to me, I was stunned. It was a beautiful moment, as Jaime played the piece with passion and intensity. As he played the last note, I realized I was so entranced by the moment, I had been holding my breath for most of the song. (Rachelle)

After the concert, the four of us went to dinner. On the way to the restaurant, I asked Mary to ride with me so I could talk with her. I shared with her that I was falling deeply in love with Rachelle, and that we felt the Lord had brought us together. I told her that we would continue to seek His will and that I would ask Rachelle to marry me if we knew convincingly that, indeed, this was of the Lord. I shared this with her, because I wanted her to know that I had the best of intentions regarding Rachelle, and I wanted her to feel comfortable with all of this if things were going to move quickly, as I was anticipating they might.

Mary was very kind, encouraging, and measured in her response. She's a God-fearing woman and very spiritual, and she asked me a very insightful question: "What did you learn from your first marriage?"

I was ready with my answer: "You have to take out the trash every day." Then I explained what I meant. I said that if you let frustrations, misunderstandings, arguments, discord, and so on, build up in a relationship, over time, resentment, hurt, and unhappiness will set in. And eventually, those feelings will become so rooted that it is almost impossible to grow love, harmony, and happiness. I had learned and decided to never allow these weeds to grow or issues to go unresolved. I wanted to address anything that needed to be addressed so that the relationship could thrive and grow.

I also told her that I recognized that my relationship with God was not what it should have been during the time leading up to my divorce, and that if I had been anchored in Christ, it would have been a different story. And I told her that I am committed to putting God first and foremost in my life every day. She then asked if I had a temper and if I was a jealous guy. I told her that I certainly had a temper, but that I have learned to channel that temper to my violin playing and not to take it out on people. And I also shared with her that I don't have a jealous bone in my body. Jealousy is a terrible thing and is glaringly indicative of insecurity. My *modus operandi* in dealing with people is that, while examining everything, I am going to trust them until they prove that I shouldn't. We didn't have a lot of time to talk further, but she felt comfortable with me pursuing Rachelle, and we agreed to have many more conversations as time went by.

> *While Jaime and my mom were in his rental car talking, my youngest sister, Marina, and I were in my mom's car talking. As we drove to the restaurant, I asked Marina what she thought of Jaime and of the possibility of us entering into a serious relationship so quickly. Marina, who was sixteen going on thirty-six, is an observant and insightful young woman. She told me she could see that this was a different experience for me than when I had dated before. She understood that when God is involved, sometimes there is no explaining how fast things can happen and how quickly hearts can be healed and united. (Rachelle)*

The next morning I had three services to play for at Back Mountain Harvest Assembly in Trucksville, Pennsylvania. This is the church of a good friend, Carlton Houck, whom I've known for a number of years. He's quite involved in prison ministry and has always supported and promoted my music ministry. Any time I'm in his area, he's always found churches where I can minister.

From there, Rachelle and I headed to the Paterson, New Jersey, First Baptist Church for the final concert of the weekend. Pastor Bill Jackson and the congregation welcomed us to the church, and we had a blessed time. Pastor Jackson encouraged us to continue to seek the Lord and told us that when something is of the Lord, He will bless. We shouldn't worry, he said, about how long the process might take. He said that three months after he met his wife, they were married and had been married happily for decades.

That was the day I told Rachelle that I loved her for the first time. I'll never forget the huge grin on her face when I said those words! I had been praying about this, and I felt that when I knew in my heart that I loved her I was going to tell her so. Saying goodbye that evening wasn't easy, but I knew I would be seeing her again soon. I just didn't know how soon! We drove back to Philadelphia where I caught a flight to California, my next destination for concerts, and Rachelle drove home to D.C.

> *When Jaime told me he loved me, I already knew. He was showing me with his actions, telling me with his expressions, and I could feel his love. At that moment, I was flooded with feelings of peace and happiness. Even though I was not yet ready to say the same thing to him, I knew I already cared for him very deeply and that our hearts had a powerfully magnetic pull toward each other. (Rachelle)*

I had nine presentations in Northern California from December 9 to 16 in Red Bluff, Auburn, Pleasant Hill, Ukiah, Angwin, Anderson, Redding, and Napa. The schedule was packed. But despite how busy and tired I was, everything was going beautifully! The Lord was blessing the concerts and people's hearts were being touched. Audiences were responding heartily, and my relationship with Rachelle was blooming. Part of the time I was in California I had the opportunity of staying with my friends Sam and Gwen Ocampo. Sam and I took advantage of every opportunity to have breakfast, lunch, or dinner and enjoy good conversation.

On Tuesday night, Rachelle announced that she would really like to see me that weekend! I didn't waste any time. Although I didn't have a lot of frequent flier miles at that moment—I had used most of them to bring many of the participants to the November 25 concert—I had enough miles to get Rachelle a ticket. She arrived in San Francisco on Thursday night while I was doing a concert, so she took a shuttle to Napa, where Sam picked her up. We were able to stay with Sam and Gwen, which was a blessing.

That Thursday night, December 13, I told Rachelle that I wanted her to be my girlfriend, and she said Yes. I am old fashioned that way; I believe in asking to commence a dating relationship officially. I don't like it when people just assume that they're in an exclusive dating relationship. I like to ask. I didn't ask her, I *told* her, but of course she could have said No.

> *When Jaime told me that he wanted me to be his girlfriend, I said Yes without hesitation. I don't usually respond well when people tell me what to do, but I understood that Jaime worded it the way he did so that I would know how strongly he felt about me and about us. The entire week leading up to that day, after we parted in Philadelphia, we talked every day, even though my work schedule and the time difference presented some challenges. It was early in that week that I realized I loved Jaime. Each night, as I would end the call at the end of our conversation, just as I was disconnecting the call, I would whisper "I love you." Of course, he couldn't hear me, but I needed a little time to accept the fact that I was falling in love with him. I was scared to give my heart to someone again. Jaime sensed that I loved him, and he also knew I was scared. Shortly after one of the concerts in Napa, he looked at me intensely and said, "Tell me!" Immediately I knew what he meant. I closed my eyes, took a deep breath, opened my eyes, and proclaimed, "I love you!" Both of us were overwhelmed with joy! (Rachelle)*

Gwen is the president of the Ukiah Valley Medical Center, and she had invited me to play all over the hospital for the patients and staff on Thursday. It was a joy to bring smiles to those hurting and working hard, and Gwen was pleased. On Saturday night, the four of us, Sam, Gwen, Rachelle, and I, were together at a concert in Napa. Afterward we went to have dinner at Rutherford Grill, a favorite place of mine. Sam and Rachelle had the kale salad, and they loved it so much that the next day we returned for some more.

> *Earlier that day, at the morning presentation, Jaime told our story and introduced me. Then, much to my surprise, he asked me to come up and speak to the audience! I was not expecting that and wondered what I was going to say. My thoughts were moving quickly, and I knew I needed some help. I prayed and asked God to give me the words He wanted me to speak. I instantly felt at peace. Thanks to the Lord's leading and my previous experience speaking to large groups of people, it went well, and I shared something that God had placed on my heart. I sensed that God wanted me to share a bit of the story of the healing and restoration He had brought me after my divorce. As I ended the story, with tears in my eyes, I looked around the audience and saw that many people were also moved and that some had tears in their eyes.*
>
> *After Jaime finished the presentation and we greeted people in the church lobby, a lot of people thanked me for sharing such a vulnerable story and asked for prayer for the difficult things they were going through. Once again, I was humbled and blessed to be affecting people for the Lord. (Rachelle)*

Our last concert in California was Sunday morning at the First United Methodist Church of Napa. It had taken quite a long time to come up with a date for this concert; our office had been in touch with Jan Lanterman, the minister of music, for a few months. But the Lord's timing was perfect. This concert took place right after the tragic mass murder in Newtown, Connecticut, and people were hurting all around the country. The combination of Pastor Lee Neish's message along with the music and testimony touched many hearts. When I introduced Rachelle and told people that I wanted to marry her, the congregation nearly adopted us. So many kind, sweet, hospitable people came up to us afterward and told us that they could help us with anything we needed should we decide to get married in the Napa Valley! That offer was certainly tempting.

That night, Rachelle got on a red-eye flight to return home, and I stayed the night near the airport to catch my flight early on Monday to head to Texas for the last leg of the tour. It was another difficult moment, but we had joy in our hearts, knowing that God was doing a great work bringing us together. We also knew we would be able to see each other once again soon.

I arrived in Texas and got ready for the last nine presentations in Tyler, Alvarado, Abilene, De Soto, Dallas, Keene, and Waxahachie. For the concerts on the weekend, I was able to have the company of one of my closest friends, Evelyn Mastrapa. My family has known her family since we were toddlers in Cuba, and any time we are in the same area, we get together. Evelyn was free that weekend, right before heading to Orlando to spend Christmas with her family, so we were able to hang out almost the entire weekend. We aren't in constant contact, but our friendship is not dependent on space or time. Those kinds of friendships are worth more than gold.

Once again, I got the time wrong for the last concert of the season! I was off by half an hour. I arrived late at New Harmony Baptist Church in Tyler, Texas, where I'd been twice before, thinking that the concert was at 7:00 P.M. Traffic had held me up leaving Dallas, and instead of arriving in Tyler at 6:00 P.M., I got there at 6:30 P.M. Imagine my surprise when I saw the parking lot was completely full and the church jam-packed with people! Brother Robbie, the pastor (bless him!), said he wasn't worried. He knew I'd get there. And he said he wasn't going to worry, because if I didn't show up, he would just pick up a violin and do the concert himself. Of course, he was joking! It was my last public performance of the year, and the church shone brightly with lights and was spectacularly decorated with poinsettias and trees. It was a fitting and spiritual ending to the concerts of 2012.

The next morning, December 24, I flew from DFW to Roswell, New Mexico, to spend Christmas with part of my family. My uncle Leonel had recently moved to Carlsbad to work in a local hospital as the head of neurology. Upon arriving in Roswell, Leonel, Mima, and I headed to the Carlsbad Caverns. I had heard of them but had never been anywhere close. It was a gorgeous day, albeit chilly, and we had an amazing time. Maydelé wasn't able to make it, so just the three of us celebrated Christmas together. Carlsbad is kind of in the middle of nowhere, and I asked Leonel what had prompted him to move there. He told me that when he was a little kid in Cuba, he read a book about the travels of a family that visited the Carlsbad Caverns, and the book had made a big impression on him. He said that from that point on, he always dreamed of going there. One day, that dream came true when he brought his mother, my grandma "Bayba," as Maydelé and I affectionately called her, along with his daughter, Christine, to visit the caverns. This story inspired me and reminded me of the power of a dream!

On Christmas night, I went out for a long jog. I have become passionate about running, and as I jogged around the golf course all by myself during sunset, I had the opportunity to invigorate my tired body and spend time in prayer. But it was too cold, and I didn't have enough layers on me. When I woke up the next morning, I knew I had come down with a cold. My body was probably run down and exhausted from weeks of going nonstop, and the cold air and insufficient clothing did a number on me.

Mima, Leonel, and I were on our way to the Roswell airport on December 26 when American Airlines called to tell me that our flight had been canceled (the three of us were on the same flight to DFW). In fact, the rest of the day's flights out of Roswell were canceled. Because Roswell is such a small airport, all the flights for the next couple of days were already full. But this is when having a bit of travel experience comes in handy. I wasn't the only Executive Platinum flyer in the vehicle; Leonel is one too! So when I called with all our reservations, we got some serious help! Leonel was headed to Paris for the New Year, so his ticket was a bit more complicated. But as usual, American Airlines' service was tops, and the agent worked it all out for the three of us. There was a flight out of El Paso that was leaving at a time that would allow us just enough time to drive there and catch our flights. Mima and I made it home, although pretty late, and Leonel was on his way to Paris.

December 27 was my first day at home since November 26, and I had a mountain of paperwork that had accumulated. As usual, Kim arrived early, and we began tackling all the different things that needed attention. In the afternoon, Merrilee Jacobs and Paul Kennamer Jr. from Smallbox Entertainment arrived for a celebratory dinner. They, along with the rest of the crew, had done an absolutely spectacular job in the production of the video recording of the concert as well as all the other interviews, trailers, and so on, and we had planned on getting together as soon as I returned home. Paul is immensely talented, and from the beginning, his vision for this project was exactly what needed to be done. I knew I didn't have to worry about anything, because I was working with one of the best!

It was an intense day because I wanted to get absolutely everything done in order to drive down to Kennesaw, Georgia, just north of Atlanta, to visit Rachelle, who was visiting her sister Chandra and her family. I was eager to meet them, as I knew it was only going to be a matter of time before they became family. So I was there until December 29. I loved every minute of my time there, sharing with Rachelle, Chandra, her husband, Matt, and the children—Colin, Zac, and Nicky. I even went to hot yoga with Rachelle, the same hot yoga studio where I had suffered the first time in February of 2011. But somehow, I was starting to like it! Either that or I was getting used to the thought that I was going to be doing this a lot because I was going to be with Rachelle!

Jaime and I were really looking forward to seeing each other after being apart for two weeks. Since our time together in Napa, we had been able to talk or use FaceTime every day. At this point, we were more certain than ever that the Lord was leading us and blessing our relationship and that our love continued to grow daily.

Chandra and her family really enjoyed the time Jaime spent with us. One of the days he babysat two-and-a-half-year-old Zac and seven-month-old Nicky (my two youngest nephews) so that Chandra and I could go to a hot yoga class together. The kids loved hanging out with "Mr. Jaime," and my sister loved it that he gave her some free time! When we left to go to Jaime's house in Tennessee, I asked my sister what she thought. Her response: "We all think you got it right with Jaime!" (Rachelle)

We had planned to come to my house on the twenty-ninth to be there until the New Year, so Rachelle could spend time with me, family, and friends before heading to Florida for a few days of vacation. By the time we got home Saturday night, I was so sick I didn't have the energy to keep my eyes open. I hadn't told her, but I had been getting worse during those two days I was in Kennesaw and was running a constant fever. I also had a cough that was getting worse. We had talked about exchanging our Christmas gifts that night, and I had the house all decorated just for her. During one of our conversations, she had told me she loved natural, real, live Christmas trees. So out went my fake tree, and in came a real one. I wanted to surprise her with that. When we walked in the door, I said, "I have a surprise for you; the tree is real."

"I just knew it!" she replied. "Thank you so much."

So much for the element of surprise. One of the other gifts I had for her was also supposed to be a surprise. She had mentioned something in passing, and I seized upon the information. When I gave her the gift and she opened it, she said, "I just sensed you were going to get this for me, because you pay attention to what I say." As sweet a compliment as that was, I had again failed at trying to surprise her. But that's how it is. A woman's intuition is inexplicable, but right on the money.

Shortly after arriving home, I thought to myself, *I'm not sure I'm going to make it to opening the gifts. I'm so tired and sick, I need to go to bed now.* When Rachelle touched my forehead, she realized I was a furnace. She works in the natural health industry, so she is quite knowledgeable about nutrition, herbs, probiotics, natural medicine, natural remedies, and so forth. Once she saw how sick I was, she immediately put together a cocktail of liquid vitamins, minerals, and extracts. Let me tell you something. I went from feeling like I needed an IV and to sleep for a week to having the fever go away, the cough go away, my throat clear up, and my exhaustion gone. Within a couple of days, I was ready to take on the world again! It was awesome.

This was particularly important because the last item on the agenda that night was a private concert I had planned for her, and I was planning on singing to her the last song on the concert list. Of course, I'm not a singer. Every time I call and sing "Happy Birthday" to my friends, they thank me out of duty; some of them ask me not to sing again! Just the other day, I called my friend Dale Galusha from Brazil to sing (and wish him a) happy birthday. When I finished, he said, "That was awful! But thank you so much." So imagine, on top of not being a singer, having my voice shot! But the "health" cocktail she gave me cured my throat. So at almost midnight that night, I began my concert.

I had told Rachelle's mom about this private concert, and she had requested I play "Via Dolorosa." So I included that beautiful song in the lineup that consisted of classical, sacred, Christmas, and love songs. This was serious business, so I told Rachelle we should dress as if we were going out to the symphony. I gave her a private concert and finished by singing the Elvis Costello song "She," from the soundtrack of the movie *Notting Hill* with Julia Roberts and Hugh Grant. Thankfully, Rachelle didn't run away, and the concert was a hit with her!

> *What a treat it was to have a private concert! Jaime played a beautiful selection of pieces, and even though we were both exhausted and he was sick, we had the kind of energy that is fueled by true love. I was thrilled that Jaime requested formal attire. I will look for any excuse to dress up, so this was right up my alley. I wore a formal black evening dress that I had packed for the occasion, and Jaime looked very handsome in his tux. I was completely bowled over by the lengths he had gone to so that I would have a beautiful Christmas celebration. Because I was traveling for work during most of December (I got to sleep in my own bed only five days that month), and at my sister's house on Christmas Day, I had elected not to get a Christmas tree for the first time since I had moved out of my parents' house. I was feeling a little down about that, and Jaime knew it. Christmas is my favorite holiday, and I had really missed decorating my house and putting up a tree. When Jaime unveiled the live tree he had brought in just for me, I was so excited I jumped up and down and grinned like a child. The tree was magnificently decorated, and I didn't want to leave the room. In everything he did and said, Jaime continued to show me that I was special to him and that he paid attention to what I said. (Rachelle)*

The next day she prepared a delicious, healthy brunch, and we invited Kim and her boyfriend, Dwayne, and my neighbor friends, Pete and Mary Ellen Ciganovich.

When Rachelle told me she was planning to go to Florida for a few days, I made arrangements to be able to visit her there. So we had a bit of time to spend together right after New Year's Day before she returned to D.C. to go back to work and I headed to Hong Kong and South Africa. We were going to spend the next two and a half weeks apart, and it was going to be difficult. But we both shared the same joy, peace, and conviction that God had brought us together, and we knew that we were going to get through this and the other times when we would be apart.

I had already figured when I was going to ask her to marry me, but I had to take care of business first. I had to talk to her father, whom I had yet to meet in person, and ask for her hand. I was also planning on talking to her mom, Mary. Since her parents divorced many years ago, I felt I should also ask her mom's permission. And, of course, I had to get the ring. During those days we spent together in Florida, I took her to a store so that I could get an idea of what she liked. Once I found out, I contacted Kevin Lawler, the general manager of the

Jared Galleria in Knoxville. Kevin had helped me a number of times in the past with gift selections and had become a friend. I told him that I was pressed for time, and he told me he would do whatever had to be done to make this happen within the time frame needed. Friendship is more valuable than money! So before I left for Asia, we got the wheels rolling.

Every day I was in Hong Kong and South Africa, no matter how challenging it was because of the time change—Hong Kong was twelve hours ahead of home and South Africa six—Rachelle and I spent time talking and praying on FaceTime or Skype. One night, the Wi-Fi signal in the room at the lodge in South Africa wasn't reaching inside. So I went outside. The mosquitoes had a powwow, a potluck, a buffet, a barbeque, and a fish fry all at the same time, compliments of my flesh. But I didn't notice it until the end. I was talking to my love!

I had a missionary concert in Hong Kong at the Hong Kong Visual Arts Centre, where a number of visitors came. The Lord blessed the efforts of Brother John "JoJo" Rey Vallejera, a missionary to Hong Kong and China as well as the rest of the team.

On Saturday night, January 12, 2013, I flew from Hong Kong to Johannesburg, South Africa, and arrived Sunday morning. I met my friend Ilsa and we flew to Richards Bay for the much anticipated safari. Ilsa is like a sister to me, and we both enjoyed the experience immensely. Every morning and afternoon the ranger would take our group out to the reserve to look for wildlife. Our group was composed pretty much of four people—Keith and Kit, a young couple from Massachusetts, and Ilsa and me. Our first day out we saw giraffes, elephants, zebras, impalas, nyalas, warthogs, monkeys, buffalos, rhinos, and a cheetah. We were just a few feet from the cheetah, an incredible animal, and he didn't even flinch at our presence.

Philemon, our ranger, was an experienced, knowledgeable, gentle soul who took great care in sharing with us the minutest details about everything we saw. Every day he would take us on what seemed to be a totally new, different trail. We'd see some of the same animals, and then some new ones, like the huge hippo, the small mongoose, and a number of magnificent birds.

Our reserve had a small herd of elephants—two sisters and a young calf. One day we found the younger sister and the calf grazing just off the path. The ever adventurous, but measured Philemon drove us close to them as they were gently grazing. The older sister was far enough away that we couldn't see her, but we could hear her chomping on a small tree. After a while, big sister came to join the other two. We were there for a few minutes without incident. All of a sudden big sister elephant looked at us the wrong way and came toward us slowly. With her trunk, she pushed against the bumper of the Land Cruiser and gently shoved us back. I was thrilled, and Keith was sweating. I guess she had decided we were too close. After the Land Cruiser rolled backwards a few feet, she stopped pushing. But then she decided we still weren't far enough away from the herd or the calf, and she came toward us again, pushing a little harder. Philemon got the cue and started the Land Cruiser. We backed out of there and left!

The next day we found the elephant herd close to the fence adjacent to the next reserve, Phinda Game Reserve. But as we got close, big sister started trumpeting and stomping. So we backed off. The elephants walked on by, and we followed from a distance. All of a sudden big sister charged us with a vengeance. I was cheering, and Keith was voicing his discomfort and desire to disappear. We were never in any danger, as we were pretty far away. But the elephant chased after us, making a straight line. As she galloped, if there was a tree in her path, she didn't go around it. She would knock it down as if it were a shrub. To see that kind of raw power was quite awesome! The next day I decided to stay in the room for the afternoon tour. It was hot, and I wanted to take a nap. When Ilsa came back, she had a fantastic story. Philemon took the group back to the fence, and they had caught the younger elephant sister flirting across the electric fence with one of the male elephants from the other reserve. The two reached way over the fence and touched trunks. I guess they were doing the equivalent of humans holding hands. And big sister didn't want humans around to watch all that flirting!

This was when, frustrated at my lack of inspiration for writing this book or even negotiating a book title, I asked Ilsa for her input, and she suggested the idea of *Crescendo* for the title. Sometimes, I don't know what I want when it comes to a song, art, furniture, decorations, choices, and so on, but I do know what I *don't* want. But when I see what I'm looking for, it hits me hard! As soon as Ilsa shared the idea with me, I *knew* this was the title of the book! Just like that, my creative juices began to flow and I started writing.

On Wednesday, we had arranged to go the other reserve, Phinda, in hopes of seeing lions. Our reserve didn't have any. Phinda was a huge reserve with more than fifty-six thousand acres and several prides of lions. I had looked forward to this moment for as long as I could remember. Our ranger and guide told us we might not get to see them, as nothing was guaranteed. But they would do their best to find them. My heart palpitated with anticipation and excitement. We were fortunate and blessed, because we found a pride of lions within an hour of beginning our adventure. Woo-hoo! They had eaten fairly recently and were just lying around peacefully by the side of the road. I had tears in my eyes. To be just a few feet away from these majestic, powerful, and dangerous beasts was surreal. I had goose bumps. I couldn't help but pray and thank God for allowing me to fulfill a dream. I hugged Ilsa, and she could sense what I was experiencing. Of course, she was going through it herself.

Anything and everything else we saw, including a massive bull elephant, was just icing on the cake after witnessing these lions. We even saw a cheetah up on the side of the mountain, in a position to scout out her next prey.

At sunset, our group, the usual four plus two British and South African couples, were taken to a beautiful, perfect mountain ridge where we overlooked a large valley just as the sun began to dip below the horizon as our hosts fed us a light snack. It was a glorious, spiritual experience. Everyone was jovial as we rode in the van on the way back to Zulu Nyala. Our British and South African mates were quite buzzed from imbibing alcohol during a snack. They began singing one of those loopy songs that seem to go on forever. The rest of us joined in.

On Friday, our last day there, Ilsa and I went on excursions both morning and afternoon. Just as we were about to head back to the lodge for dinner, we saw something awesome and gruesome at the same time—a cheetah going on a kill with her two cubs to teach them the art of hunting. There was a large herd of impalas, with a young one that sat on the grass without moving much. *Something doesn't seem right,* I thought to myself as I watched it. Soon after, I saw the cheetah squatting down about fifty feet behind the herd. Suddenly she took off like a bullet. The entire herd of impalas, on instinct, had already begun to flee—except for the young impala who still hadn't moved. By the time it began to run, the cheetah stepped right in front of it, swatted it, and held it for her cubs to come and finish the kill. The herd of impalas, safely across the road, turned back and called and called and called to the young impala, who never came. After a minute, the impala herd then dashed off. Momma cheetah choked the impala, as the cubs began to eat it.

By this time, literally all the Land Cruisers carrying groups of guests had surrounded the scene. I say it was an awesome scene because it was nature at work. But it was also gruesome because an animal lost its life. I was reminded of Romans 6:23: "For the wages of sin is death, but the gift of God is eternal life through Jesus Christ our Lord." This world is filled with sorrow and pain. Our only hope is Jesus Christ, the gift of salvation that He has purchased with His blood, and His soon return to take us home!

Ilsa photographing me trying to get close to a giraffe.

With the lazy cats in the background.

With our guide Philemon, along with Ilsa and Kit on an excursion.

CHAPTER 18

CRESCENDO

{Growing; Progressively Louder}

Upon returning home on January 21, I had just a couple of days before hitting the road again for nearly a month. I was so exhausted and jet-lagged that I slept all the next day and all the following night. Early on January 23, I drove down to Newnan, Georgia, to spend the day playing at one of the hospital facilities of CTCA. What a privilege it was for me to play music that brought comfort and perhaps healing to those affected by cancer. What a ministry it is to reach out to people who are sick. I had never seen such complete, gentle, and loving care from the entire staff. They were there truly to minister to people. I am honored to be associated with such a top-notch organization that is doing so much to treat the whole person—body, mind, and soul.

The next day I flew to Washington, D.C., to visit Rachelle as well as to prepare for a number of concerts in the area. When she picked me up, it was an emotional reunion. We had been apart for two and a half weeks, but it seemed like months. I was getting to the point that I couldn't stand to be without her, and we asked the Lord to guide us in order to do His will and be able to be together on a regular and permanent basis. The Lord had healed our broken hearts and was putting love in our hearts like we never imagined could happen again. But God is in the business of making miracles happen, and we shouldn't be surprised about that! We just have to trust Him and follow His will for our lives.

Little did Rachelle know that I had the ring with me. It would have to remain hidden for a couple of weeks, and I could barely contain my excitement and anticipation! On Sunday afternoon, January 27, we headed to Chambersburg, Pennsylvania, to spend the evening with Rachelle's mom, sister, and two brothers. I was going to meet Anthony and Justin for the first time, and on Monday, I planned to ask Mary for permission to marry Rachelle. They had waited for Rachelle and me to join them in order to open all the Christmas gifts. So, in essence, we had Christmas on January 27. Fabulous! I was invited to play some Christmas songs on the violin, which I happily did. We ate pizza and had a fantastic time!

The next day, as Rachelle was doing some work downstairs, I sat down to talk to Mary for what I thought would be a short conversation. Mary and I had communicated a few times before (I had told her ahead of time about my private concert for Rachelle after Christmas; I called her while in South Africa and told her my plans for how, when, and where to ask Rachelle to marry me, etc.). We seemed to be on the same page. For these reasons, I thought she would quickly give me her blessing and permission to marry her daughter. An hour and a half later, it was time to leave, and I still didn't have the green light. I was disappointed, but I understood that Mary wanted to leave no stone unturned. She asked me a number of questions. I answered them. But having watched her daughter go through a devastating divorce, she was, of course, reticent to give her blessing, especially when our relationship had progressed fairly quickly.

Mary told me she'd like to take some time to pray and have another conversation with me. And so even though I didn't leave having fulfilled my objective, I put it in the Lord's hands. The Lord wasn't going to show Mary something different than He had shown Rachelle and me. I was a little anxious, because the following weekend on Super Bowl Sunday I was to talk to Mr. Richard, Rachelle's dad, and ask him for Rachelle's hand. I was hoping to be able to tell him that Mary had already given her blessing. I say I was a little anxious, because it was a bit bold of me to meet him for the first time and a day later ask him for permission to marry his daughter! So away we went.

The way I figured it, I would spend some time getting to know Mr. Richard and his wife, Mary (not to be confused with his ex-wife and Rachelle's mom, Mary), and perhaps on Monday, I would ask to speak with him.

Sometime Sunday afternoon Rachelle went into the kitchen to bake her dad his favorite cake, and his wife went upstairs. I had a pretty good idea what I wanted to share with him but hadn't put the whole thing together in my mind. As we sat there, perhaps thirty minutes before the Super Bowl began, he turned and said, "I hear you have something you want to ask me. So why don't you step into my office? We can talk, and then we can watch the game." All of a sudden I froze. All of a sudden the guy who had gotten up to play in front of many people in many different places and on different stages, just plain froze! It's hilarious now, but I was pretty nervous at that moment.

I didn't know Mr. Richard well, but I had grown to respect him from the things Rachelle told me about him. He is a loving father, an upright gentleman, and had served his country. He was a Green Beret in the U.S. Army Special Forces during Vietnam. Though I had nothing to be afraid of, I was nervous. It was probably excitement. He shared with me how his daughters were his joy and that all he wanted was for me to love Rachelle with all my heart and treat her right. We had a lengthy conversation, and at times I had a tear flow from my eye. I grew to love him on the spot as he shared with me a bit about his life, and I caught a glimpse of his influence in Rachelle's life and how he was partly responsible for rearing a truly amazing woman! When he finished talking, he said, "Welcome to the family, son! From now on, you're my son." He has called me that ever since, and I call him Dad Rick.

As you can imagine, the rest of the evening was a breeze. We watched the Super Bowl together, but my heart and mind were far away. I was crawling out of my skin thinking about asking Rachelle to marry me. I wished the next couple of weeks would fly past so that moment would arrive! But I still had to hear from Rachelle's mom. I had told her, like I had told Dad Rick, that I didn't just want her permission, I also wanted her blessing. Since Rachelle is very close to her siblings, I also talked with Chandra and Stephanie to tell them I wanted to marry Rachelle and that I hoped to receive their blessing, which they granted. So only Mamá María was left!

> It was great fun introducing Jaime to the rest of my family. Everyone loved him right away! They could all see that he loved me unselfishly, was committed to having a Christ-centered relationship, and that I was able to completely be myself around him. Despite the fact that our relationship had progressed so quickly, my family seemed at ease with things and welcomed Jaime with open arms. (Rachelle)

Since September 2012, the days had been going by so fast, it seemed the clock had been rigged to go twice its normal speed: my regular concert and travel schedule, the preparations for the November 25 concert, the Christmas tour, and the surprise turn of events with Rachelle had flown by. But now, the days inched along.

I had planned on the eve of Valentine's Day as the time I would ask Rachelle to marry me. Trying to throw her off, I had joked with her for weeks that I was wanting to propose by May. Then I said maybe in April or perhaps even by the end of March. She has such an acute sixth sense that I was hoping she wouldn't figure it out. She told me later that she tried to bury the antennas by not even thinking about when I might propose, so that it would be a surprise.

I had suggested that instead of celebrating Valentine's Day on February 14, we beat the crowds by celebrating the night before. On Friday, the fifteenth, very early in the morning, we were going to fly to Portland for a marketing seminar cosponsored by Pacific Press®, the publisher of this book, to put on a concert for the bookstore managers and promote the new DVD and this autobiography. So it made perfect sense to have our special date on February 13 in the evening.

I planned on taking Rachelle to dinner in D.C., and then for us to walk around a couple of monuments. Then I would ask her. The weather had been impetuous and unpredictable, but it was supposed to be balmy that day. Instead, it got cold and rainy. That morning, after we met for hot yoga (yes, I acquiesced and began going with her regularly when I was visiting her in the D.C. area), as I drove her to her apartment, it was just miserable outside: the sky was completely gray, the temperature had dropped, and it was raining. She said, "Honey, if it's still ugly tonight, do you want to leave the walk around the monuments for tomorrow?"

If I had said No, that I wanted to push forward with our original plans, regardless of the weather, she might have suspected something. So I said nonchalantly, "Sure, sweetheart! We can just leave it for tomorrow or another time." But in my head I was thinking, *There is* no way *I'm not going to propose tonight!* So I prayed for better weather.

After trying to reach Mamá María since Monday, I finally got to talk to her that afternoon. She told me she had been praying about this decision since I had left, and that just recently she had felt a direct impression from the Lord. She shared with me these words:*

> *Dear Jaime,*
> *The Lord said to Moses, "This how you are to bless the Israelites," and I pray this is what He has said to me. I believe it is.*
> *"Tell Jaime and Rachelle, this is how you are to bless them." Numbers 6:24–26:*
>
> > *"The* LORD *bless you*
> > *and keep you,*
> > *The* LORD *make his face shine upon you*
> > *and be gracious to you;*
> > *The* LORD *turn his face toward you*
> > *and give you peace."* †
>
> And so I bless you, Jaime Jorge, to marry my precious firstborn child, my beloved daughter, Rachelle.
> *And with this blessing and your song "The Little Drummer Boy," the Lord has given me these further words to bless you as you ask for my daughter's hand in marriage this night.*
> *May you dance through life with my daughter with the same passion with which you play the violin.*

---

*   See the appendix "Dinner With Jaime," for more details about this blessing and the reaction of Rachelle's mom to our relationship.

†   All Bible quotations are from the NIV.

May you always play " 'O Sole Mio" for Rachelle with the glorious joy and love, yet ever more each day, that I saw and felt at the concert where you publicly declared your intentions towards my daughter.

May you dance through your marriage to Rachelle with the same lively and adventurous heart, soul, and body-stirring beat as that of "The Little Drummer Boy."

May my daughter tell me every day, as she did today, that she is 1,000 percent sure she wants to be married to you, and may her countenance show every day that she is being loved by you with every fiber of your being, and may she in turn be open like a rose in full bloom with her face to the sun, basking in the glory of your love for her as you submit and surrender more and more each day to the Lordship of our Savior, Jesus Christ, as He gives you all you need to love my daughter as He loves the church; as she is given the freedom in her heart—that is unlocked by your love for her—to love and respect you with all that is in her.

May you always remember this command that Paul gave in Ephesians 5:25–33.

May Galatians 2:20, 21 give you the strength to follow Him and fully surrender to Him.

May you wear the full armor of God every day as the angel spoke to Daniel in Daniel 10:19, "Oh man highly esteemed. . . . Peace! Be strong now; be strong." Ephesians 6:10, 11, 14 continues, "Be strong in the Lord and in his mighty power. Put on the full armor of God so you can take your stand against the devil's schemes. . . . Stand firm then, with the belt of truth buckled around your waist, with the breastplate of righteousness in place" to love and honor my daughter Rachelle to the fullest of your ability in His strength; and in turn to fully receive the glorious gift of her complete love, honor, and respect given from Him, in Him. (Please read all of Ephesians 6 to Rachelle.)

And so, having said these things to a man who is "wild at heart" and who is serving, following, and seeking after his "wild at heart" God:

Jaime Jorge, you have my blessing and my permission to marry my precious firstborn child and beloved daughter, Rachelle. Guard her tenderly with your life.

Mamá María

My heart pounded with elation, and tears of joy flowed freely down my cheeks. I had her blessing!

That evening it was drizzling when I picked up Rachelle to go on our date. She took my breath away when I saw her! I had reservations at a marvelous Italian restaurant, Tosca, right in the heart of D.C. I remember that the place was absolutely full during dinner, but beyond that, I can't remember what I ate or much of anything else, except Rachelle. My heart was bursting with joy and love, and we shared a magical dinner.

After dinner, we discussed whether to end the evening there or proceed with our plans. We both agreed that the weather wasn't so crummy, so we would go to the Lincoln Memorial. President Abraham Lincoln is my favorite president, and his memorial is the place I had chosen to propose. Here's a man who stood up to the injustice of slavery and abolished it, an avid reader who was infinitely knowledgeable, a brilliant statesman and politician, and an honest, God-fearing giant who steered our country through perhaps its most critical period since achieving independence from Great Britain and certainly anything else this country has faced since.

I wanted to photograph the moment, and my good friend Amy Newman from Reading, Pennsylvania, had put me in contact with a local photographer, Marlon Correa, who worked for the *Washington Post*. He was waiting when we arrived. It was freezing cold, but I was sweating under my dress shirt. To my pleasant surprise, the Lincoln Memorial was nearly empty! The few people there when we arrived, walked down the steps of the memorial just as we walked up the steps. We basically had the whole place to ourselves! Marlon could be heard snapping pictures so that Rachelle wouldn't think anything odd was going on.

As we stood next to those tall, majestic columns at the entrance of the memorial, I asked her to stand with her back to the Washington Monument so I could take a picture of her with my iPhone. Then she took a picture of me. Then I said to her, "Honey, this gentleman is a photographer. Let me ask him if he will take a picture of both of us!" She liked the idea. So I said to Marlon, "Sir, would you be kind enough to take a picture of us on my iPhone?"

"I'd be happy to!" he replied. I was cracking up inside.

"As a matter of fact," I said, "you have a professional camera, which is much better than the one in my phone. Would you be willing to take a picture of us on your camera, and if I give you my e-mail address, would you kindly e-mail it to me?"

And he said very seriously, "I'd be delighted to do so."

Rachelle thought I was the bee's knees!

He snapped a couple of pics, and I gave him my "card" and thanked him. He handed me his card. Then, as Rachelle and I walked toward the giant statue of Lincoln sitting on a chair, I said, "Look, baby, he works for the *Washington Post*! He must be a very good photographer." I was having a great time.

As we approached the statue, I told her how much I loved the life of President Lincoln and how special it was for me to share this moment with her. I don't know how much time passed; it seemed to me like time stood still. We talked, hugged, held hands, walked around (and yes, I kissed her too), and snapped a couple more pictures of each other. Marlon was in the background, taking pictures of the whole thing!

After all this, I said, "Well, do you want to make a quick visit to the Jefferson Memorial?" She agreed, as this had been our plan all along. Then as she turned to fasten her coat, I dropped to one knee. Subtly, but frantically, I had been looking for the ring; I had forgotten which pocket it was in! Finally, I reached into the left inside pocket of my suit and slid the ring into my right index finger. When she turned around, I was on bended knee, and I said, "Baby, I love you! Will you marry me?" For a split second, she froze with her mouth open. She looked at me and then at the ring, as if perhaps this wasn't really going on. Then she jumped into my arms as she said, "YESSSSS!"

I was so excited that when I launched myself at Jaime, I think I almost knocked him over! (Rachelle)

Those moments were pure bliss. There was laughter, immeasurable joy, and excitement. I figured Marlon knew what was going on, as I could hear the click of his camera sounding off in rapid fire. But I still held out my left hand, as we continued to hug, and I gave him a big thumb's up! For the most part, I had managed to surprise her.

Jaime did finally manage to surprise me! Even though I knew he was going to ask me to marry him, because we had already discussed marriage, I didn't know when he would ask. I like being surprised, and I didn't want to know, so I actively did not think about it. The entire evening was like a beautiful dream. Once again, I was blown away by how much planning and effort Jaime had put into creating such a special moment for us. (Rachelle)

As I write this, we are planning on getting married the weekend of the Fourth of July 2013, on a beach in South Florida.

I give honor and praise to God for bringing us together. As we prepare to get married, I am asking the Lord to give me everything I need to be the woman He made me to be. Jaime and I pray that God will enable me to be the wife that Jaime needs and that God will equip Jaime to be the husband that I need. We know that through His strength, and by His grace, we will succeed and thrive. (Rachelle)

I apologize to the entire editorial, executive, and sales and marketing team of my publisher, Pacific Press®, for taking so long to get the manuscript to them, especially Jerry D. Thomas, Scott Cady, Doug Church, Russ Holt, and particularly my close friend Dale Galusha. Last year in 2012, when I agreed to write this second autobiography, I was frankly afraid, almost ill, over the commitment I had made. You see, I didn't have an ending! After my life seemed to fall apart, although I had plenty to share and talk about, I still didn't have an ending. But in a short amount of time, God chose to change all this in a very drastic and exciting way!

The frenetic pace of all of the activities of the last few months had also pushed me to the brink of exhaustion, physically, emotionally, and creatively. My brain was fried. I couldn't write. But the Lord came through. And perhaps the most amazing part is that I have this beautiful ending to share with you—the gift and blessing of God bringing Rachelle and me together.

I had announced to Mima last year that I didn't think I would ever get married again. I told her, "Mima, I have learned to be content with my life. I have the best family, the most amazing friends, a ministry that is of the Lord and that is being used by the Lord to reach many for His honor and glory, and plenty of adopted nieces and nephews around the world to spoil. I'm just going to marry my violin."

And she responded, "That's all right, my son. But always be open to God's leading and working in your life." How prophetic those words were.

God brought Rachelle into my life at just the right time. The Lord knew her qualities as a gifted former professional athlete and chef, along with her leadership skills, healthy lifestyle, and excellent ability to speak to audiences, and He has matched us together perfectly. We were both brokenhearted; God mended and healed our hearts. And I believe He is calling us to minister together. I envision a ministry in which, as part of our concerts, Rachelle can speak on the benefits of exercise, healthy eating and living, share her exercise routines and recipes (I smell a cookbook coming), and together we can encourage couples not only to stay together but also have a happy and thriving marriage. Every day Rachelle and I pray and ask God to put more love in our hearts—for Him and one another. Every day He answers our prayer. Every day we ask Him to use us in the way He wants, so that we can be powerful testimonies to His love and amazing grace!

In 2012, the Lord led me to found a nonprofit organization—Healing Music, Inc. Through this charitable organization, we want to be able to continue reaching people for Christ in Cuba where I've been so involved the last several years as well as all around the world, establish a scholarship to help young people develop their musical talents in order to use them for His honor and glory, and eventually open the Mavda García Music Academy (named after my mother) where young people can study music as well as learn the tools necessary to start their own music ministries. If the Lord impresses you to become a part of this ministry, whether by praying for us or supporting us, please feel free to contact us. Our toll-free number is 888-501-9882. You can also visit our Web site at www.jaimejorge.com and join our e-newsletter list, visit our Facebook page (Fans of Jaime Jorge), be a part of our Twitter family (@jaimejorgemusic), as well as download our app (Jaime Jorge), which is currently available for the iPhone only.

My brother or sister, I don't know what you might be going through right now in your life. Whatever it is, I have a simple message for you: please focus on Jesus

Christ. Through all my ups and downs, peaks and valleys, highs and lows, and especially through the darkest moments of my life, He was always there. He never left me. I wandered away from Him, but Jesus didn't go away. In Revelation 3:20, Jesus says, "Behold, I stand at the door and knock. If anyone hears My voice and opens the door, I will come in to him and dine with him, and he with Me." Every single day, Jesus knocks at the doors of our hearts. He wants to be Lord of our lives, and He wants to be our best Friend.

Please don't allow anything in this world, be it money, work, relationships, food, or anything else, to come between you and Jesus Christ. If you don't know Jesus as your Savior, would you accept His gift of salvation right now and ask Him to come into your heart? And if you've already accepted the gift of salvation, would you recommit your life along with me and ask Him to use you however He's planned to be a great blessing to many?

This book ends for now, but not the story. I plan on sharing another autobiography with you in the future. I don't know what's going to happen between now and then, but God knows, and I know that whatever He has in mind for you and me is better than we can ever imagine.

May God bless you. May God keep you. And may you shine for Jesus!

At the Lincoln Memorial the evening of our engagement. Photos by Marlon Correa.

DINNER WITH JAIME

I was twenty-one years old the day she was born. She was my firstborn child, and I had no idea how I would take care of her. I had never even changed a diaper that I could remember, and I felt completely inadequate to perform the daunting task of taking care of this helpless treasure nestled in my youthful arms. I needn't have worried for a moment because God had *chosen* to make me a mother, and He was very capable of performing the daunting task of making me able to care for the greatest gift He had ever given me, my precious daughter, Rachelle Marie. (Please note, dearest Chandra, Anthony, Justin, and Marina, that I say here "the greatest gift He *had* ever given me" as you other four *had* not come along yet; each one as you arrived, was equally, yet distinctively, precious in my eyes and in my heart!)

She was a beauty right from the start—one of the world's great beauties—and she captured my heart the moment she laid her little head on my shoulder. God used that moment to do what He has done from time immemorial with mothers. He infused me with a heavenly, yet earthy, dose of mother's love as I felt and looked at that tiny head resting peacefully and trustingly on my shoulder. In that instant I knew that I was well equipped for motherhood and that I would be fully capable of the task ahead. My heart was full to bursting, and I was ready for whatever was to come.

As I sat and held my baby, Rachelle, a little five-year-old boy named Jaime, across the Atlantic Ocean in the country of Cuba had also received, not long before, a great gift from God, one which he also did not yet know how he would care for. It was the gift of a violin and the talent to play it in a way that would change his life and the lives of the many people who would come to hear him play with a passion that would stir their souls for God and His purpose for their lives. We can all thank God for the gift that He gave this little boy, and thank his mother for being up to the task that God gave her to foster this gift in her son. And oh, how he would need that mother's love, encouragement, sacrifice, determination, and firmness in the years to come. As Jaimito practiced his violin (at the age of five, this was due, no doubt to his mother's diligent supervision!) on that beautiful June day in 1975, little did he know that thirty-four years later the beauty that had just captured her mother's heart would, for a fleeting moment, capture his heart, as her eyes locked with his while he played the violin on the stage of her church. Three years later, that same beauty would come back into his life in a way he had never imagined and capture his heart for good this time.

I know these things about Jaime, because some of them he has told me in talks we have had, some of them I have witnessed with my own eyes, and some of them I have heard him tell about in his concerts. Thirty-seven years after the birth of my precious daughter Rachelle, I am very excited and well pleased that she is going to marry Jaime and that he is going to be part of our family as my new son. However, Jaime Jorge was not always my favorite person. In fact, when I first met him I was very suspicious of him and of his intentions toward my daughter.

Rachelle and I live about two hours apart—she in Washington, D.C., and I in Chambersburg, Pennsylvania. When she first told me that a friend was coming to the D.C. area to do some violin concerts and asked if I would like to come to one, I thought it might be nice and that my sixteen-year-old daughter, Marina, might enjoy it because she had just taken up the violin. With my busy schedule, finding room for a violin concert by an artist unknown to me or to Marina was not at the top of my list. But getting a chance to spend time with Rachelle and getting together with my oldest and youngest for some mother, daughter, and sister time greatly appealed to me. However, after double-checking the date, we realized that Marina, a ballet dancer, would not be able to make the concert, because she was performing that same day. So it would just be a date with my oldest.

In the meantime, Rachelle's seemingly distant acquaintance and friend, Jaime, the concert violinist, whom she had not seen in ages and whose name I had only heard mentioned once about three years before, was suddenly going on a run with her and all of her church ladies at the crack of dawn on the morning of the concert! Then after the run, the two of them were off to a hot yoga class followed by a sumptuous pre-concert brunch! In all fairness, I must say that I was invited to all of these activities, but not being a runner or a hot yoga aficionado, I chose to attend only the easy one, the delicious brunch—all 105 pounds of me!

However, my radar was up that a musician who travels all around the world was passing through town and seemed to be just a bit more than interested in my daughter. *What man,* I thought to myself, *who keeps as busy a schedule as Jaime Jorge does with his evening concerts, invites himself out for a run in the still-dark hours of the morning with a whole gaggle of ladies, unless he is very interested in a certain one? What man would put himself through a hot yoga class (105–110 degrees worth of hot!) that he is not used to, right after a run the day he is giving a concert, unless he is very interested? All this before the concert, and brunch with her mother to boot?* The man had a plan! I was not born yesterday, and I wondered, *Who is this Jaime Jorge guy, and where in the world did he come from?* He seemed to have just popped out of the woodwork, and I had the feeling he was not going to go away without a fight. I just had a feeling!

I must say that when God infused me with that mother love on the day of Rachelle's birth, along with it came eyes in the back of my head, a very special discernment, a voice that would make suitors think twice about how they would treat my girls, and the courage to put those suitors in their places when needed. I had just walked through some very serious heartaches with Rachelle and was not inclined to think that a new relationship was the best thing for her at that time. But Rachelle insisted that she and Jaime were just friends, that there was nothing more on her end, and that Jaime respected this totally. I thought, *OK, beautiful girl, this whole 'we are just friends' thing never works for the guys like it does for us girls, especially when he is dealing with a girl like you. But let's see what happens. I'll meet him, and we'll just see!*

I did not know what to expect in a concert violinist, and never having heard Rachelle talk about him except in passing a few years earlier, I had a very vague picture in my mind of someone nondescript, a bit rumpled and frumpy maybe, a bit out of shape and probably not able to keep up with Rachelle—maybe not even her ladies in the upcoming run. I did not envision him as being someone who would be her type. The whole "we're just friends" thing usually evokes this type of a picture! Yet, somehow I felt that my vague impression might be wrong and that he could very well be quite dashing and sweep us both off of our feet (I speak of myself in the sense that as a mother I could get fooled; I had been before, as had my mother before me when she let a high school boy take me out after he had "swept her off her feet" with his charm. In reality he was a snake, the worst boy I ever dated, and as a mother I have tried to remember that lesson. But still, a charming man is a charming man, and a mother, no matter how watchful, can get fooled.) Once again, I had this feeling that there was more here than Rachelle or I could begin to fathom. It was just an inkling, but it was there.

The day before the concert, I arrived at Rachelle's for our weekend together. The next day I had a luxuriously lazy morning while she and Jaime slaved away running and doing hot yoga. I must say I had worked up quite an appetite for our brunch by the time Rachelle staggered in, dripping with sweat and as red as a beet from all her exertions. Actually, I must let it be known that Rachelle, being a world-class athlete, never staggers, and that as a courtesy to Jaime and the fact that he had a concert that night, the run they did that morning was just a tune-up to what she normally does. I believe the more appropriate term would be that Rachelle came sailing in and breezed past me calling out, "We have to leave for brunch in fifteen minutes. I'll just grab a quick shower. Jaime is on a tight schedule. You *are* almost ready, aren't you?"

My heart sank, because I am never ready on time but never cease to hope and try! I had thought surely it would take her longer than fifteen minutes to get ready. How *does* she do it? And she would look amazing, as always, I knew.

I was on pins and needles as I rushed to finish getting ready for this brunch, which I sensed was more important than either of us could realize. I wanted to look nice also, because a prospective suitor, when meeting a girl's mother, should be able to see how nicely the girl will age. It is an old wives' tale, but one that every mother teaches her son, and there is some truth to it! I say *suitor* here because, regardless of the nonsense that Rachelle was feeding me (and which she had talked herself into believing) about Jaime being just a friend, in my eyes, he was a suitor, nondescript though I might have imagined him to be. And he would later prove me very right, indeed!

I did manage to throw myself together just in the nick of time for Rachelle to announce that she was ready. I was right, she did look amazing, and off we went to the restaurant to meet with Jaime Jorge. I wondered what he would be like and wondered if he could possibly be good enough for my daughter. Even if he were, I knew she was not ready for anything but friendship. Still, I just had a feeling.

When we arrived at the restaurant, Jaime walked out to meet us in the outdoor seating area. He was tall enough and good looking enough, and very fit and athletic, which I was not expecting for a violin player. He was definitely not rumpled or frumpy, and he did not fit the "we are just friends" vague impression that I had cooked up in the back of my mind. Not at all, but at the same time, I did not get the sense right away that he was Rachelle's type. I thought maybe after this concert he would go off traveling around the world some more, and Rachelle might not mention him again until the next time he had a concert in the area, maybe in another three years. Jaime, however, had other ideas, as I soon found out. Jaime was friendly, charming, and easy to talk with; the three of us had a fabulous time sitting outdoors on a warm day in early November. Our waiter was a dear little fellow who seemed to be from Japan, spoke very little English, and left us scratching our heads as to why he was working in a French restaurant when he did not seem to speak a word of French, nor did he seem to speak a word of English for that matter. Jaime's sense of humor was put to the test immediately as Rachelle and I attempted to do what we always do when ordering, and that is to modify, modify, modify! We have both worked in the restaurant business at many different times in our lives. We know what we want and aren't afraid to ask for it;

we know it can be done if properly communicated to the server. Our dear little fellow on the other hand (the waiter, not Jaime) was having none of it. He let us know in no uncertain terms that there would be no modifications happening on his watch. He would protect himself from the ogres in the kitchen at all costs by refusing our requests to add spinach and a luscious-sounding tomato creation to our omelets or to substitute a more exotic cheese for the one listed on the menu for that particular omelet. It simply could not be done; the chefs would not budge, he insisted. But I am convinced that the man had no idea what he was refusing because he could not understand us, and he couldn't possibly communicate to the kitchen what he could not understand. He was such a dear little man that Rachelle could not bear to make things difficult for him by insisting he talk to the chefs and ask if her requests could indeed be honored, so she proceeded to outfox him by ordering side dishes of all the things she had wanted to add to her omelet. Our waiter, never suspecting a thing, happily smiled and benevolently nodded his consent to all of Rachelle's side orders. Off he trotted to the kitchen, wiping his brow, smiling happily. I have no doubt that he was breathing a huge sigh of relief that he had skirted the language barrier once again and that he would not have to face the terrors of communicating to the kitchen our outlandish requests for modifications of their sublime creations.

Meanwhile, my "mother's radar" had picked up on the fact that Jaime was gazing at Rachelle with quite a bit of admiration as she expertly dealt with our stubborn little waiter. (In my mind, he had gone from "dear" to "stubborn" at this point.) I believe Jaime appreciated being in the company of such a beautiful woman who knew how to think on her feet. He obviously got quite a kick out the hilarious proceedings, and I believe he had already recognized that Rachelle is a very resourceful girl who knows how to communicate and get results. As I later found out during one of our talks, Jaime had a list, and I believe on that day, in that little French restaurant with the obstinate little waiter, right under the ever watchful eyes of her mother, Jaime Jorge was quickly coming to the conclusion that this beauty just might fit his whole list!

We all had a lot of fun with the whole scenario, and Jaime's sense of humor was refreshing to see and experience. I had no idea just how much of a sense of humor he really has, but I was soon to find out, because Jaime was not going anywhere. Oh no, Jaime was here to stay, but I did not know this yet! As we waited for our food, I had the opportunity to observe the chemistry between Jaime and Rachelle, and I had no doubt that he was more than interested—and she knew it too. We women always do! But he is a musician who travels all around the world, and as I happened to notice what appeared to be some texting under the table here and there by Jaime, I wondered how much he was really enjoying our company. I must say that where technology is concerned, and as far as the rules of social media go, I am living in the Dark Ages but I still subscribe to the outdated theory that texting at the table is rude. It is safe to say that I was not impressed by this, and it gave me pause to wonder.

We did not wait long before our waiter brought the food. The omelets and the side dishes were fabulous, well worth what we had to go through to get them! The three of us had a wonderful conversation as Jaime answered my many questions about his music and gallantly listened to the observations and advice of a woman (yours truly) who knew he had to be good, but who had no idea (yet) that she was dealing with a well-known, world-class violinist. To Jaime's credit, there was no hint of a condescending air to him; looking back, knowing what I know now, I am deeply impressed at his humility then, and I continue to be so right up to the present time.

As Rachelle and I walked back to her apartment after brunch, Jaime walked right along with us, even though he had been starting to get a little concerned about the time needed to get back to his hotel to practice and prepare himself for the concert. He clearly did not want to let Rachelle out of his sight until the last possible moment, and I wondered if he was going to be able to get ready in time, much less be able to have time to practice. Finally, he did reluctantly break away from us to get to his car that was "on the way"—I never believed that for a second!

Rachelle and I arrived at the concert in plenty of time to get good seats; as I listened to Jaime play for the first time, it began to dawn on me that this man was very good—very, very good. (Actually, I realized it the moment he began to play.) Certainly, he had not needed the well-intentioned help I had tried to give him earlier at brunch about venues and churches where he should try to book more concerts. In my opinion, he must have people beating down his door and begging him to come to their church or venue to play for them. Jaime played with a passion I had never seen or experienced. I was mesmerized by the beauty of the music emanating from his violin as he lovingly coaxed the sometimes hauntingly beautiful, sometimes lively, and always perfect, notes out of his instrument. Jaime plays not only with his fingers and his bow, but with a myriad of facial expressions that add so much to the beauty of his playing—it displays his passion for his violin and takes the listener to another level in the experience of hearing and seeing him play his instrument. I think the best way to describe it is to say that Jaime becomes one with his violin as he plays. He uses every part of himself to coax out the glorious notes, and his face beautifully reflects this effort as well as the joy that he feels as he plays; of this there can be no doubt as one experiences Jaime and his violin in concert.

As the concert progressed, there was something else of which there could be no doubt. My daughter noticed and felt the same things I did, but on an even deeper level, as I believe the first stirrings of something more than friendship began to blossom in her heart. As I sneaked a peak at her face from time to time, I saw a peace, a glow, and a sureness of God's love washing over her as she listened to Jaime use the gift God gave him. That night, I believe she began to get a vision of who Jaime really is, and who he could become to her. This vision was unformed and was not even a twinkle in her eye yet, but Jaime already had plans. Jaime knew the vision; his vision was big enough for both of them until Rachelle's vision and feelings could become clear to her with God's help. There was a current of electricity flowing between Rachelle and Jaime, and oh, how her mother could see it and feel it! Unbeknownst to me, that current was more tangible than I had realized as I came to find out that the man sent her text messages during intermission. Rachelle clearly enjoyed the attention as she read her messages. Then before the intermission was over, she had a visit from Jaime at her seat as he presented her with a copy of his book, complete with a personal note inside.

What are this man's intentions? I asked myself as I thought about what she had just been through in the last few years. I was feeling just a tad bit protective and suspicious, and I wondered, *Does he text and present signed books with personal notes to pretty women all around the world during his concerts? He may be a Christian violinist, but he is still a man, and a pretty good-looking one, at that.*

A mother has got to look out for her daughter! I told myself, as I began to mildly speculate. *Does he have a girl in every port?*

This mother could clearly see that the man was a very good musician who was being used by God to touch people's hearts and proclaim the gospel to them. But I did not yet know his heart, and I wondered what his intentions were. But Jaime knew. He knew something yet to be revealed to Rachelle and to me, and he would reveal it soon.

After the concert, Jaime sat at his table to meet and greet the concertgoers and help to sell his CDs, DVDs and books. Rachelle and I went through the line, and I had loved his music so much and had been so blessed by it that I wanted to buy everything! I noticed that Rachelle also was picking out quite a few things and that she was arguing with Jaime about paying for her CDs as he was insisting they were a gift from him.

Hmmm, I thought, *Are there other beautiful girls in other "ports" to whom he is giving away his CDs after concerts?* Did I say I was suspicious? Indeed I did, and my suspicions were mounting. He just seemed to be much too interested for his intentions to be just friendship. He seemed to be moving much too quickly for this to be a genuine interest in one woman, and I was forming the suspicion that he might be a bit of a player, not necessarily in any kind of sinful way, but just not something that Rachelle needed. I must say that by the end of the concert, after having watched and heard Jaime play and speak, I believed that he had a sincere heart for the Lord and his ministry, but he was still a man, single, uncommitted at that, and there were a lot of pretty women on that road around the world! After what I had just walked through with Rachelle, I just did not think she should be one of them at that time, no matter how innocent it all might be.

There were a lot of people at the concert and Jaime was very busy, but we did not think that after the day Rachelle had spent with him it would be appropriate to just leave without saying goodbye and giving him a chance to talk with us if he so desired. And it appeared that he did so desire as I noticed that no matter how busy he was, who he was talking with, getting pictures taken with, or signing his autograph for, he seemed to always be aware of where Rachelle was. I took note that Rachelle seemed to be equally aware of Jaime's presence and that she was quite aware also that his focus was on her.

Rachelle and I had made plans to go out for dinner after the concert, and we had planned for it to be the birthday dinner that I had owed her, just a few months late. As anxious as we were to have this long-awaited birthday dinner, just the two of us, we both looked at each other and said, "Should we invite Jaime?" And we both said, "Yes." I was definitely feeling the afterglow of the beauty of the gift of music that Jaime had just bestowed on us, and he *was* beginning to grow on me. Rachelle approached his table as things were winding down for him and asked him if he would like to join us for dinner. It did not take Jaime long to respond with a resounding "Yes." I could tell he was quite pleased with the invitation, to put it mildly, as he confesses to his audience every time he now tells the story. (I *love* that part of the story as Jaime practically does jumping jacks to demonstrate to the audience what he was feeling inside when Rachelle asked him to join us for dinner. I just *love* it!)

Once the invitation was issued, Jaime wasted no time in packing up the last of his things. And taking charge beautifully, he escorted us to a lovely Cuban restaurant for an experience none of us will ever forget. We arrived at Cubano's and were welcomed warmly even though it was quite late. The host ushered us to our table where Jaime and Rachelle sat on one side and I sat across from them. Jaime was in his element, exchanging rapid-fire Spanish with our waiter, as he ordered dish after dish of different types of Cuban food for Rachelle and me to try. We were having a wonderful time, enjoying ourselves quite a bit. I was complimenting Jaime on the beauty of his violin, still not completely aware just how good this man really is, just how large his gift is. Praise God He gifted him with humility also! Jaime was charming and attentive but much too attentive, I was beginning to think, as I watched his arm go across the back of my daughter's chair in what I thought was a rather familiar and possessive manner. I had let my mother's guard down a bit in the afterglow of the concert, and my radar immediately went back up.

Whoa! Whoa! I thought to myself. *What is this guy doing? They are supposed to be just friends, and even if they aren't, he is behaving in a way that is much too familiar for such a short time.* I really began to speculate on the girl-in-every-port theory again, when the next thing I knew, Jaime tried to feed Rachelle one of the delicacies he had ordered for us to sample. If I hadn't known better, I would have thought that he and Rachelle were quite an item, except for the fact that Rachelle was having none of it as she leaned away from the arm across her chair and would have no part of his trying to feed her the Cuban delicacies. In the meantime, I was feeling that my earlier worst suspicions were being confirmed. *He is a player,* I thought. *He does have a girl in every port! Well, over my dead body will my daughter be one of them!*

Jaime would go on to prove me wrong and more than redeem himself in my eyes during a later talk with an explanation for his behavior that night; but for the moment, this mama was in full protection mode! And so, as Rachelle practically fell out of her chair (to hear Jaime's version of the story) to avoid the arm across it, and as she turned her face away from the solicitous Cuban gentleman trying to feed her delicious tidbits of Cuban delights (that would be Jaime, not the waiter), I did what any good mother would do. I tried to diffuse the situation. I leaned in and began to engage Jaime with all sorts of questions and conversation to try and find out more about him, what his true intentions might be, and to try and rescue my daughter from this man, who in my eyes at that moment was being far too familiar! And I continued to ask myself, *What* is *this guy doing?*

In Jaime's defense, I later found out that there was quite a bit more history (just friends) between them than I was aware of and that Jaime regretted letting Rachelle get away several years earlier before anything could even begin with them, and had already determined he was not going to let her get away again. As he told me in that later conversation, "It was all over for me not long after we got to the restaurant; I knew she was the one for me." Jaime loves to exaggerate every time he tells the story of our dinner, and each time it gets funnier and more outlandish. As Jaime's version of the story goes now, Rachelle was practically on the floor trying to avoid his arm across her chair, with her nose up in the air refusing the proffered delicacies, and I am lying across the table trying to talk to him to get his attention away from my daughter while entertaining my unfounded suspicions of his having a "girl in every port."

All of this notwithstanding, we all had a wonderful time, the food was fabulous, and Jaime really was the perfect gentleman. As the evening came to an end, Jaime walked us to our car, and I thought, *Maybe now, he'll go back to traveling around the world.* But I had a feeling at this point that maybe he was serious, that Rachelle was more to him than just a girl in this port, especially when he invited Rachelle to come to his twenty-fifth anniversary concert in Chattanooga and invited my daughter Marina and me to come also. I was excited and knew this would be a special night for all of us.

After we said Goodbye and got in the car, I looked straight at Rachelle and said, "Girlfriend, you are in trouble!"

She looked straight back at me and said, "I know!"

Meanwhile across the parking lot, as was revealed to me in that later conversation, Jaime told me he got in his car and said to himself, *Jaime, you are in trouble!* As all three of us thought about all the trouble Jaime and Rachelle were in, God had other ideas as He was putting together His plan for a match made in heaven.

After that night, Rachelle began to share with me that although Jaime had indeed gone off globetrotting again with his violin, he was beginning to pursue her long distance with lots of phone calls and texts. She shared with me many things that they talked about and many things about Jaime himself that were increasingly chipping away at my suspicions and impressing me more each day. The long-distance relationship continued to grow slowly but intensely at the same time, I believe. Before long it was time for a very special night—the twenty-fifth anniversary concert. It was a glorious event and had been beautifully planned by Jaime and his staff. Rachelle was drop-dead stunning in a new dress and heels that put the rest of us to shame, and we were nothing to sneeze at to be sure! We found out later that although Jaime had gotten us our VIP tickets, unfortunately he did not know where we were since it was open seating in the VIP area. Throughout the night, he searched the crowd for a glimpse of Rachelle, but he could not find her, which may have been good because otherwise he might not have been able to concentrate on the task at hand. Rachelle, on the other hand, had only one thing to concentrate on, and that, of course, was Jaime and the inspired music he was making with the other gifted musicians. A number of times I looked over at Rachelle and saw that her face was glowing with a radiance. Jaime may not have been able to find her, but she had found him, and the depth of joy on her face as she watched and listened to him was something I had never seen before. My heart soared for her, and it was scared too! *Oh Lord, please protect her and protect what is happening between them. Oh Lord, let it be real, and let it be completely of You,* I prayed fervently, inspired by the heavenly music of Jaime's violin.

As I watched and listened to Jaime play his violin with such skill and passion, I marveled at the gift God had given him and that I was so privileged to be able to soak up all of this beauty surrounding me as one gifted and blessed musician after another came onstage to play and sing with Jaime. It was a magical night for us, and I believe it was a turning point in Rachelle's feelings for Jaime. I believe that night and the following day, which they spent together talking deeply, is when God truly blessed her with the knowledge, not fully formed, but there nonetheless, that this man was the one for her. Not too long after the anniversary concert, Rachelle called me to talk and with great certainty, lightness, and sheer glee, said, "Mom, don't be surprised if I end up marrying that man." A few short weeks later, she said to me, "Mom, I think I am going to marry that man!" I was slowly but surely being won over by what I saw in my daughter as a result of the care of this man. Who could stay suspicious? And yet, it was all so sudden and moved so fast.

Another night she called, and as we talked I heard her voice ringing with something I had not heard in a long time and something more that I had never heard before: a softness, a sweetness, a surrender to a growing love and passion she could never have dreamed of, a love and passion grounded in the One who had made them for each other and who had brought them together in His perfect time. Oh, how I pray it is so!

Rachelle told me in that joyous voice that I was becoming accustomed to hearing that Jaime had told her something absolutely beautiful and that it would make me very happy. I was, of course, very concerned at how quickly things were moving and was anxious to hear what she had to say. She told me that she and

Jaime had been talking for hours, and I could tell that she was floating on air. I will never forget what she told me; and to this day, what he said and the action behind those words have given me the confidence and faith that Jaime Jorge is indeed "the real deal," as my daughter Chandra was the first to profess. (Chandra is the family sage, filled with unavoidable perception and insight; when she speaks, one listens! She is sparing with her compliments, and I have never heard her use these words before about anyone!) Here is what Rachelle said to me on the phone that night: "Mom, Jaime told me tonight that he believes that it is a man's job to make a woman feel so safe and so comfortable that she can trust him enough to open up and place her heart in his hands. He said that he believes it is the man's job to take care of her heart so well that she feels safe enough to tell him anything and to be who she really is. Mom I am impressed, really impressed."

I had to admit that I, too, was very impressed and highly encouraged. But at that point it was so early on that I told her I would have to see that action behind those words before I could trust that he lived by them. I wanted her to be careful too; it was so soon! But I *was* impressed, and I *was* beginning to cave. Yet, it was much too soon for me to let down my guard for my daughter, and it was all happening so quickly.

As I continued to watch the relationship grow, taking on wings like eagles, swiftly soaring ever higher with every call from Jaime after the first concert in D.C., and then even more so after the twenty-fifth anniversary concert, I continued to caution Rachelle in my frequent talks with her about getting involved with Jaime so quickly after her breakup.

I told her that she needed to be very careful about making Jaime her confidant and helper as she broke the chains of bondage created by this very difficult and yet at times beautiful relationship she had just come out of. She agreed with me and said she would be careful, yet I could not have foreseen how quickly things would progress or that Jaime would move into the position that I had feared and advised Rachelle against. I believe now that I need not have worried, because Jaime was and is up to the task. I have come to believe he was sent from God to help Rachelle break free and fully come into the glory of the love God had prepared for Jaime and her.

Not long after this conversation with Rachelle, I attended my third Jaime Jorge concert and received a shock and surprise. I was also able to have a beautiful talk with Jaime that began to reassure me that he was indeed "the real deal."

Jaime's Christmas concert—my third and Marina's second—was held about three hours from our home. We had gotten his Christmas CD and were looking forward with great excitement to hearing all of our favorite songs performed live. When we got there, Jaime surprised us by greeting us personally at the door with a warm hug. Not only that, but he ushered us to our seats as well! More melting of this mother's heart! Rachelle joined us, and about halfway through the concert, we got quite a surprise, as I mentioned above. Jaime began to talk, and said, "Something wonderful has happened." I realized immediately that he was going to tell the audience about Rachelle. He told them of his relationship with Rachelle and how it had progressed so quickly. He spoke with such passion and humility, love and excitement that my heart melted even more toward him and the relationship.

When he was almost finished, he held out his arm toward Rachelle and said in a voice ringing with great emotion, "And *if* she will let me, I will marry her." He was speaking of a future time, and I was greatly relieved, because at this point I had begun to fear he was going to propose on the spot! I felt that it was far too soon for a proposal, to be sure. I could see the emotion in both of them and the great joy and openness that Jaime showed us all. And once again, my heart melted and softened even more that a great work was being done by God. Jaime then dedicated "'O Sole Mio" to Rachelle and proceeded to play it with the grandest passion I have ever seen or heard. I was deeply moved and was truly blessed to watch both of them and their joy as he played the love song for her. I will never again be complacent when I hear that song, although there will never be another rendition like that one for me! My ever watchful mother's heart was concerned once again because I knew that anyone who is capable of such passion and emotion when playing music could very well have a temper. I filed that thought away to express at the appropriate time. I wanted Rachelle to have her eyes open and to be aware of what life could be like with a musician and his emotions. I would get my chance to speak of this much sooner than I had anticipated, and it would not be with Rachelle.

The four of us had dinner plans after the concert, and Jaime asked if I could ride with him, and Marina ride with Rachelle. I knew Jaime wanted to talk to me, and I was impressed by his courage. He told me he had wanted to talk to me before the concert about how he felt about Rachelle, but there was not enough time. He revealed to me why he came on so strongly with Rachelle that first night we had dinner. He told me about himself, his history, and most importantly, his relationship with Rachelle from the first time he saw her in the crowd at a concert, how he was struck by her beauty, her eyes, and felt a connection. He let me know that he felt God had brought him back into Rachelle's life to be the strength she needed to break completely free from the relationship that God was calling her out of. He said some very profound things concerning this subject, and I just knew God was leading him and that he truly loved my daughter with Christ's love.

He showed humility while admitting to have been proud a few years back when Rachelle did not respond to him as he had expected her to. He said that he knew he had made a big mistake and that was why he had behaved as he did at that first dinner—he was not going to let her get away again! Well, he certainly did not. Here he was telling me that his intentions were indeed to marry my daughter and that he would be asking my permission and blessing in the future. But for now, he said, he would be patient and wait until Rachelle was ready to make that step.

I felt compelled to ask Jaime if he knew why he was divorced and what he had learned from his first marriage. There was no hesitation at all on his part. He said Yes, that he absolutely knew. "I learned that you have to take out the trash every day." I knew immediately what he meant, and a more perfect analogy I have never heard. He went on to explain that he meant you cannot let things fester; you must address then every day.

Jaime had said to Rachelle, "It is a man's job to make a woman feel so safe and so comfortable that she can trust him enough to open up and place her heart in his hands." He said that he believed it is the man's responsibility to take care of the woman's heart so well that she feels safe enough to tell him anything and to be who she really is. I was, and continue to be, beyond impressed by what he had learned and how he continues to apply it in his relationship with my daughter. As we talked more that night, I told him about the concern I had felt during the concert and asked him if he had a temper. He laughed and said Yes, but that it is never directed at the women he loves and that I could ask his mother and his sister if I didn't believe him.

It was a wonderful talk and the beginning of a wonderfully open relationship that I have been able to begin to develop with Jaime and he with me, as he often includes me in his plans of surprises for Rachelle as well as many other things. It was also the beginning of a new phase in their courtship as things now began to move in the definite direction of marriage, while still allowing Rachelle the time she needed to be ready for that step. Jaime has thanked me many times for what he says was a great question about what he had learned from his earlier marriage and that it has made him think even more deeply about it and apply what he has learned. He has not let me forget that I asked him if he had a temper and teases me about it from time to time. Well, a mother has got to look out for her girls, and this mother was especially looking out for her girl who needed some extra special "looking out for" at this point in her life.

In November 2012, when Jaime arrived in D.C. out of the blue, or so it seemed to me, Rachelle had just come out of a very serious, difficult, and heart-breaking relationship. Three years earlier she had suffered the devastation of an unwanted separation, culminating in divorce a year later. As I walked with her through these difficult times, we developed a deeper mother-daughter bond than we ever had before. Rachelle learned to trust my counsel, and I believe she came to a deeper understanding of the innate wisdom and love of a mother (no matter how old her child is) and how much she needed that from me even though she was all grown up. Those were difficult and dreadfully painful times, yet they were times filled with the joy of a mother and a daughter knowing that we had each other and that most importantly we had God to guide us. Through all of this Rachelle came to appreciate more than ever the important role of her parents and their discernment in her life as a grown woman. I have told Rachelle and all of my grown children many times, "I do not want to run your life. I am not interested in running your life. All I want to do is to be able to impart my wisdom to you, to have you listen, and then do what you think is best." I think Rachelle has always understood this, but when Jaime came so suddenly to the forefront of her life after so much heartache, she understood in a new way just how valuable her family's input was, as we hashed out together if this guy was for real or not. It did not take long to begin to see that he was, indeed, for real and that he had other ideas than Rachelle or I had on that morning in November when we met Jaime for brunch at that little French restaurant. And his ideas were good, very, very good. He did not ride off into the sunset but continued to pursue my daughter with patience, gentleness, passion, and love while communicating to me his honorable intentions all along the way. In doing so, Jaime impressed me yet again with his willingness to be an open book and reassure a concerned mother who wanted the best for her daughter and who was not yet convinced that Jaime Jorge's sudden appearance on the scene (so it seemed) was what was best for her at that time.

As her relationship with Jaime began to blossom and then hit warp speed, Rachelle involved me in a way that she never had with other relationships, a very appropriate way that honored me as her mother and allowed me to share my wisdom with her as she had never before allowed me to do in so much depth. I believe that God is showering blessings on Jaime and her because of the honor they both have given to me and to her father, and also to Jaime's parents, as their relationship has progressed.

It has been very rewarding for me to be able to be by Rachelle's side at the beginning of her relationship with Jaime. As I watched with concern what seemed, at first, to be a man moving too fast, I heard each day from Rachelle—her voice filled with joy—about the things that were being discussed between the two of them. That gave me reassurance that even though the relationship was moving so fast, God was in it.

Jaime has encouraged Rachelle to share the progression of their relationship with me in the talks she and I have had alone and in the many talks the three of us have had, and continue to have, over the phone. I often get a call from the two of them and have the delightful privilege of being regaled with the many details of the progression of their relationship with lots of fun romantic details that just warm a mother's heart. That Jaime not only would want to do this, but more often than not is the instigator of these detail-filled calls, has been another way he has been able to show me that he is the real deal.

I have always believed that a parent's appropriate involvement in his or her child's choice of a mate is a very healthy and valuable tool in knowing who is that right one. The fifth commandment says, "Honor your father and your mother, that your days may be long upon the land which the LORD your God is giving you" (Exodus 20:12). This is the only commandment with a promise attached to it, and it is profound. Parents have so much insight into their children and can often see things their offspring cannot see in the grand and glorious blindness that comes with the first dose of romantic love. For this purpose alone, as well as a myriad of other things, the honor given a parent can bring greater rewards than can be imagined in this modern world of "I did it my way." I see Jaime and Rachelle living out this commandment as their relationship grows ever stronger in God and as they seek out the wisdom of their respective parents and future in-laws.

True to what I have just said, and true to his promise, Jaime did ask me on January 28 for my permission and blessing to marry my daughter Rachelle. We had several more wonderful talks over the phone, just the two of us, in which he shared many things with me regarding his intentions and how he felt about Rachelle. Each conversation gave me more trust and confidence. One very important thing that he shared with me was that Rachelle had said to him that she had never fully surrendered herself to a man until Jaime. She said, "Jaime, you are completely surrendered to God, and that is why I can do this." Another beautiful thing that set my heart even more at ease was when Jaime told me, "My love grows for Rachelle every day. Every day I think, *I can't love this girl any more.'* Then I do." These things and many others were on my mind when Jaime showed me the exquisite ring he had made for Rachelle and asked for my permission and blessing to marry my daughter and answered more of my questions. His answers were what I wanted to hear and gave me great hope.

Even so, it had all happened so fast, and my mother's heart needed to absorb more and to seek the Lord's sign that this was truly of Him. I felt quite sure that it was, but I needed to hear a final and certain Yes from the Lord. Jaime was very patient and let me know that he planned to ask Rachelle on February 13. We parted with the agreement that I would seek final confirmation from God and give Jaime his answer when I had received mine from God.

During the next two weeks, I prayed and asked God to reveal to me whether I was to truly give Jaime my blessing and my permission to marry my daughter, and if so to please show me the blessing I was to give Jaime.

On February 9, just four days before Jaime wanted to propose to Rachelle in front of the Lincoln Memorial in Washington, D.C., I attended a Michael W. Smith concert. Near the end of the concert, Michael spoke at length to the audience about the love of God, and when he had finished he told us he wanted to give us a blessing. I felt chills go through me at the word *blessing*. "Oh Lord," I said, "You are going to do it again, aren't You?" Michael then stretched his hands out over the audience in a blessing and spoke these words over us:

> "The LORD bless you and keep you;
> The LORD make His face shine upon you,
> And be gracious to you;
> The LORD lift up His countenance upon you,
> And give you peace."

This, of course, is Numbers 6:24–26, one of my favorite scripture verses. In that moment I knew that God had given me the sign I had asked for to confirm that He truly was in this relationship between Jaime and my daughter, that it was of Him, and that He had given me the blessing for Jaime and for Rachelle. I knew I needed to write a blessing in my own words that God would give to me to add to the Bible verse from Numbers. And He did. The words just came pouring out of me so quickly that I could barely get them written down in time. I was able to get it written before Jaime called me on the phone and asked for my final permission and blessing. We had a beautiful talk in which I told him the story about getting the sign and blessing from God. Then I gave him the blessing and gave my permission to Jaime Jorge to marry my daughter Rachelle Marie.

Jaime was emotional, and he thanked me for the blessing. I told him I would e-mail it to him so he could read it to Rachelle. This blessing is inspired by God, given to me by God, just as I believe God is the Source of the love Rachelle and Jaime have for each other. May it always be so, and may they every day love each other more than the day before with the love of Adam and Eve.

The Blessing:

Dear Jaime,
The Lord said to Moses, "The is how you are to bless the Israelites,"
and I pray this is what He has said to me. I believe it is.
"Tell Jaime and Rachelle, this is how you are to bless them" Numbers
6:24–26:

> *"The L*ORD* bless you*
> *and keep you,*
> *The L*ORD* make his face shine upon you*
> *and be gracious to you;*
> *The L*ORD* turn his face toward you*
> *and give you peace."**

And so I bless you, Jaime Jorge, to marry my precious firstborn child, my beloved daughter, Rachelle.
And with this blessing and your song "The Little Drummer Boy,"
the Lord has given me these further words to bless you as you ask for my
daughter's hand in marriage this night.
May you dance through life with my daughter with the same passion
with which you play the violin.
May you always play " 'O Sole Mio" for Rachelle with the glorious
joy and love, yet ever more each day, that I saw and felt at the concert

---

* All scripture quotations in this blessing are from the NIV.

where you publicly declared your intentions towards my daughter.

May you dance through your marriage to Rachelle with the same lively and adventurous heart, soul, and body-stirring beat as that of "The Little Drummer Boy."

May my daughter tell me every day, as she did today, that she is 1,000 percent *sure she wants to be married to you, and may her countenance show every day that she is being loved by you with every fiber of your being, and may she in turn be open like a rose in full bloom with her face to the sun, basking in the glory of your love for her as you submit and surrender more and more each day to the Lordship of our Savior, Jesus Christ, as He gives you all you need to love my daughter as He loves the church; as she is given the freedom in her heart—that is unlocked by your love for her—to love and respect you with all that is in her.*

May you always remember this command that Paul gave in Ephesians 5:25–33.

May Galatians 2:20, 21 give you the strength to follow Him and fully surrender to Him.

May you wear the full armor of God every day as the angel spoke to Daniel in Daniel 10:19, "Oh man highly esteemed. . . . Peace! Be strong now; be strong." Ephesians 6:10, 11, 14 continues, "Be strong in the Lord and in his mighty power. Put on the full armor of God so you can take your stand against the devil's schemes. . . . Stand firm then with the belt of truth buckled around your waist, with the breastplate of righteousness in place" to love and honor my daughter Rachelle to the fullest of your ability in His strength; and in turn to fully receive the glorious gift of her complete love, honor, and respect given from Him, in Him. (Please read all of Ephesians 6 to Rachelle.)

And so, having said these things to a man who is "wild at heart" and who is serving, following, and seeking after his "wild at heart" God:

Jaime Jorge, you have my blessing and my permission to marry my precious firstborn child and beloved daughter, Rachelle. Guard her tenderly with your life.

All my love,

Mamá María